CREATIVE MINISTRIES

CREATIVE
MINISTRIES

✠

David F. Marshall, Editor

Pilgrim Press   *Philadelphia/Boston*

Library of Congress Catalog Card Number: 68–8396

Chapters 1–5 and 9–11 are reprinted with revisions from articles that appeared in the *United Church Herald,* and are used by permission. Chapter 3 also appears in Gabriel Fackre, *Secular Impact: The Promise of Mission* (Philadelphia: Pilgrim Press, 1968).

Chapter 7 is reprinted from *Together,* January 1965. Copyright © 1965 by The Methodist Publishing House.

To Mart for giving me the chance, to Frank for help and advice, and to the Rev. Robert C. Waters *for his candid and lasting introduction to the concept of creative ministry, not in ideas but in person.*

PREFACE

✠

Much has been written in the past decade on the future of the local church. Successes in new, experimental ministries have been pointed to as the future wave of church life. The local church on the corner has been pointed to as "captive" to its society, as possibly—some would add "with the grace of God"—on its way out as the influential force in Christian life.

The local pastors and churchmen, feeling threatened by the new, experimental—what this book calls "creative"—ministries, have taken pains to point out that these ministries derive most of their financial support from the local churches. As one layman locally prominent in his church once said to me, "If it weren't for our support, those guys wouldn't be able to minister at all, much less experiment."

This rivalry has created a false division in most persons' minds about creative ministries. On the one hand, there is the local church with its building, its familiar program, and its time-tested methods. On the other hand, there are the experimental, new, creative ministries which exist without buildings, sometimes without set programs or mapped-out structures. It has been falsely felt that these two are antitheses of each other, that these two types of ministry are different in kind.

The purpose of this book is to put the lie to such an assertion. The book hopes to establish that the local church on the corner and the night minister walking his beat have almost exactly the same thing in common. What they hold in common is their ministry, their creativity in facing the situation and in hoping to make way for solutions provided by the Holy Spirit. By this, I do not mean that all local churches and that all creative ministries, for that matter, are sharers in a common grace. Far, far from it. There are local churches which are so close to the cliché and the caricature that they deserve their criticism, and perhaps they deserve more criticism than they are now receiving. There are also experimental, new ministries which are so disposed in their attitude and their actions that they deserve every crass remark made about them.

This book has selected several creative ministries which have shown themselves to be not only oriented toward the local church, but actually in a reciprocal relationship with local churches. There are local churches included in these creative ministries, because what the churches and the ministries share is a common style of approaching a problem.

This book hopes to prove, through giving examples, that there are not local churches on one side and experimental, new ministries on the other, but that there are creative styles of ministry and there are uncreative styles of ministry. It is this second polarization which demands criticism, and not the various institutions.

After you have had a chance to work through the various examples and the several chapters on theology demanded by the examples as necessary correctives, you will be able to see more what is meant in making the split not between institutions but between styles of ministry.

In looking ahead, it is hoped that you will be able to appreciate the difference in approaching the problem through a criticism of style. For now, the task is examining several examples of creative ministry with style in mind. Truman B. Douglass, executive vice-president of the United Church Board for Homeland Ministries, begins with his introduction on the typology of various creative ministries.

David F. Marshall

CONTENTS

✠

INTRODUCTION

✠

We have had some difficulty knowing how to designate the new forms of ministry that have been developing during the past dozen years. We began by calling them "experimental" ministries. This seemed too pretentious. They are not experimental in the scientific meaning of the word. We have not been able to begin with a precisely defined hypothesis to be tested, and move to carefully controlled experiments for testing it, and then evaluate our results by the application of exact, quantitative methods. After recognizing these deficiencies and after considering several other options, we finally settled on the general term "new forms of ministry."

Yet there is a sense in which the ministries we shall consider *are* experimental. They are attempts to help the church break out of its religious ghetto. They are attempts to help the church find ways of healing the wide rift that runs through its life today— a rift which is not between confessional positions or theories of church policy, but which is between the men of the future and the men of the past. They are an endeavor to enable the church to add to its role of being the community of memory, the role of being the community of hope. Whether the contemporary church has the skills and the energy to attain these purposes is still an open question; and to the extent that the new ministries throw light upon their achievability, they are indeed experimental.

Nevertheless, we have decided to adopt the more modest appellation "new ministries." Even this may be somewhat questionable. Some of these creative ministries have their forerunners in work which has been done in the British Isles and on the European continent. Some of them have developed by an evolutionary process out of enterprises the church has been carrying on for a long while. Most of them, I suspect, have their real prototypes in the New Testament. They are "new" mainly from the standpoint of their contrast with a frozen and stereotyped form of church life which developed in nineteenth-century America and has carried over well into the second half of the twentieth century. This form is too constricted to contain the vitalities of Christian life today.

In the past it has been thought that the only way to insert something radically new into the church was by the process of fission—

division; and so we have had the continuous rape of the unity of the church and the appearance of new denominations.

We have noted a more serious breach of unity—the fact that so many of the most authentically Christian movements of our time have felt obliged to move entirely outside the church in order to find freedom to make their witness and fulfill their vocation. Many of these vital Christian movements which grew up outside the church have been unable to find hospitality within its doors.

Both of these trends constitute one type of incentive behind the search for new forms.

A second type of observation is that the church is so often the major obstacle in the way of its own renewal.

We have longed for a structure of church life which enables the whole people of God to assume responsibility for the church's witness and mission. Yet even our so-called "free churches" are still riddled with clericalism and expect the minister to be the missionary in behalf of the congregation.

We have hoped to enter into creative dialogue with the world. Yet our principal medium of communication is the sermon—the monologue—which answers questions nobody is asking instead of raising questions that need to be discussed.

We mouth slogans such as "structure follows function," and recognize the dependence of the mission on the structures of the mission. Yet we complacently perpetuate church structures which, for instance, partition responsibility for metropolitan New York among several ecclesiastical authorities and which divide our planetary society, although it is bound together by a common humanity, an interdependent economy, satellite communications, and a common threat of total extinction, between "homeland" and "world" ministries.

Can there be any doubt that the church needs to insert into this picture something authentically "new"?

What are these new forms of ministry, and how extensive are they? Do these creative forms of ministry arrange themselves according to certain types that can be classified?

A year or so ago I developed a fairly simple typology for describing the new ministries. Let me attempt, therefore, a swift description of what is going on in this area.

1. I begin with what I am calling *ministries of reinforcement.* These are the least radical of the new forms of ministry—the least radical in principle, that is, although they may be very radical in performance. In this type of creative ministry we accept the va-

lidity of purposes which people have defined for themselves and then try to help them toward the realization of those purposes.

For example, in southern Georgia, churches and a foundation are supporting a School of Citizenship Education. This is primarily designed to help Negroes exercise their constitutional right to the ballot. But to exercise this right in the Deep South they must be able to pass literacy tests and show some acquaintance with the ways of a more sophisticated culture than the one to which they are accustomed. So in these schools Negro people of all age-groups are taught such things as the elements of reading, writing, and comprehension; how to register to vote; how to open a bank account and draw a check; how to negotiate with the landlord before signing a sharecropper's contract; the simple bookkeeping necessary to recognize whether they are being cheated; and where to go for legal aid.

The men and women who take the courses in this school are given the responsibility of organizing similar schools for their neighbors—in Georgia, Alabama, Mississippi, and Louisiana. As a result there have sometimes been as many as two hundred of these Schools of Citizenship Education operating simultaneously in the Deep South.

Helping people to achieve their own purposes—especially purposes as democratic as exercising their rights of citizenship—does not seem a very radical objective. But in some parts of our country the degree of acceptability of helpfulness is determined by whom you help. When you are helping people whose self-reliance and dignity are a threat to the existing power structure, you are being radical. When you are helping people to avoid being cheated when there are elements in the community who consider themselves as possessing a God-given right to cheat Negroes, then you are being very radical indeed. When you are teaching Negroes to put their money in the bank instead of entrusting it to "massa" without any accounting, then you are planting land mines under the foundations of a parochial civilization.

This has been the situation with the Child Development Group in Mississippi. When adults began to participate with the children in the program of fundamental education being carried on there, they began to ask questions. When the children were taught lessons in basic human rights, the adults raised questions about their own human rights. When Negroes began to raise these questions, people like Senator James O. Eastland and Senator John Stennis of Mississippi were disturbed. When Senators Eastland and Stennis were disturbed, they alarmed the national administration about its chances of rebuilding the old-line Democratic Party in Mississippi. When the Democratic administration was alarmed, it began to express its uneasiness to the Office of Economic Opportunity that financed the Child Development Group in Mississippi. When the churches attempted to articulate the needs and hopes of the children of Mississippi, they found themselves in the middle of a fierce and highly complicated power conflict.

To try to support some of our fellow citizens in their endeavor to better the lot of the most deprived children in the most deprived part of America would seem to be a simple and straightforward kind of Christian ministry. It has proved to be quite otherwise. Yet the church intends to continue with it.

2. A second new form of ministry may be called the *ministry of dialogue*. There are some groups within our culture with whom the church has little communication. They have their own patterns of thought, their own closed system of values, their own standards of competence and status. One such group is the community of scientists. In some ways this community resembles the church, because they both tend to be self-contained and closed.

For several summers two front-rank theologians, Dr. Harvey Cox and the Rev. Joseph Duffey, have stationed themselves at a conference center at Woods Hole, Massachusetts. This community is significant as a gathering place for scientists. Here are located an oceanographic institute, a marine biological laboratory, and the headquarters of the National Science Foundation. Because of this clustering of scientific enterprises, many scientists choose Woods Hole on Cape Cod as a summer vacation spot. Through the planning and leadership of Dr. Cox and Mr. Duffey, it was possible to engage these workers in the physical and biological sciences in encounters with persons who are occupied in struggling with major social issues such as civil rights, international affairs, and the effects of urbanization. The purpose was to work toward the humanization of the scientists by engaging them in dialogue dealing with questions of human meaning and purposes—concerns which often seem quite outside the concerns of workers in these sciences.

3. There are *ministries of service in new areas*. How does the church enter the new worlds of twentieth-century man as a servant community?

There is, for example, the new world of leisure. What is the church's responsibility in connection with the new fact that millions of Americans have access to large segments of leisure time? The National Council of Churches has a ministry in the National

Parks. Each year during the past several summers more than fifty young ministers and theological students have been involved in this ministry. Several other ministries to people engaged in leisure and recreation have been initiated—to the skiers on the ski slopes of Oregon, California, Colorado, and Vermont; and to vacationers in such a place as Las Vegas, Nevada. Task forces are studying the theological and ethical implications of the new leisure. A motion picture has been produced by the church which graphically states the questions the new leisure poses for our whole culture.

The church has scarcely begun to take account of the meaning of the leisure revolution. It has been said that you can tell more about the dissolution of a civilization by what people do with their leisure than by what they do with their work. In the area of leisure, many signs indicate that we are at the beginning of a process similar to the one which came to its fulfillment in the fall of the Roman Empire. Is it possible for the church to help in reversing this trend toward the misspending and destructive uses of the gift of free time which has been so painfully won by mankind? Surely this is one of the major challenges we face. It may shake our conventional work ethic to its foundations.

4. A fourth kind of new ministries may be called the *ministries of exploration*, which are largely characterized by looking and listening. The French call them ministries of presence. The church, through some representative or group of representatives, is simply present in the area of need. It is not there for any ulterior purpose. In being present it cultivates its own sensitivity to the human issues at stake and responds to human needs in any way that its new sensitivities direct.

The churches' earliest ventures with new, creative ministries were of this sort. They are generally well-known, and I shall not describe them here. They would include the first conscious undertaking in a new form of ministry—at the Bread and Wine Mission in San Francisco, the original home of the beatniks, where some communication was established with the strange new forms of revolt which have come to dominate so much of our youth culture. They would include the ministry on the Strip in Las Vegas, Nevada, where we tried to come to some kind of terms with the equally strange culture that has developed around the gambling resort industry.

5. In addition to these there is a long list of new ministries which I find it difficult to classify—generally because each of them combines several of the types I have previously mentioned. I will call attention only to a few.

I think of ministers of metropolitan mission, who operate out-side the structure of the local parish but who help local parishes and groups of parishes understand the meaning of our urbanized society and the demand which it presents to the Christian church.

I think of the attempts to enable the church to strip down for its missionary task—in a suburb of Denver, Colorado, for example, where for seven or eight years a congregation has been demonstrating that it can be authentically a church, with an effective mission, without the encumbrance of a church building. I think of the development in the new city of Columbia, Maryland, where thirteen denominations (with the close cooperation of the Roman Catholic Archdiocese of Baltimore) are united in sustaining a group of ministers who serve all the participating communions, and who work together in providing physical facilities which belong to the whole group rather than to any single denomination. I think of the numerous ventures toward updating the church's ministry, both clerical and lay—the Urban Training Centers in Chicago, San Francisco, and New York; the ecumenical center for the Renewal of the Church in Town and Country at Merom, Indiana; the Laboratory for Leadership and Learning in Christian Education at Lancaster, Pennsylvania. Then there are more comprehensive ecumenical endeavors, such as the one in the inner city of Kansas City, which involves the United Church, the Presbyterian Church, and the Roman Catholic Church.

Are these new forms of ministry evidences of a hankering for novelty or of an authentic search for church renewal?

I must answer in all honesty that I think both possibilities exist. A church may become so preoccupied with the unconventional or the seemingly new that it neglects its basic ministries—communicating the faith; nurturing the young; ministering in understanding, compassion, and love to individual persons in all sorts and conditions of life; building a community of love and trust in which the natural barriers between man and man and between group and group are broken down through the common acknowledgment of a sovereign Father-God. The new ministries are not to be substituted for the essential tasks of proclaiming and teaching the faith, gathering people into a Christ-centered fellowship, and transforming this fellowship into a missionary community engaged in service to the world.

Sometimes a particular form of new ministry may take on the character of a fad. There was a time when I thought that almost every congregation which was baffled in finding a relevant form of service solved the problem by starting a coffeehouse (see chapter two). There are now several hundred coffeehouse ministries scattered around the country. I do not think anyone is likely to prove anything we do not know by starting another one.

Granting our propensity for being overfascinated by the novel, and our tendency to turn what once seemed a good idea into a fad, I would still insist that the burden of proof must be carried by the old rather than the new. Say the best that you can for our tried-and-true ways; many of them are obviously tired, otiose, stiff-jointed, shopworn, sterile, disconnected from the issues of real life, remote from "where the action is." Consider the key words of New Testament faith: the Holy Spirit, conversion, regeneration, death, and resurrection. They are all terms of creativity, of newness of life, and this certainly means a renewal of structures and forms of ministry.

An article by Professor Michael Novak of Stanford University in *Daedalus, The Journal of the American Academy of Arts and Sciences* (Winter, 1967) is entitled "Christianity: Renewed or Slowly Abandoned?" This seems to me an accurate statement of the true alternative we face. It is not the sharp alternative of "Christianity vs. Communism," or "Christianity vs. Secularism," or some other simplistic "versus." It is rather the alternative of "Christianity: Renewed or Slowly Abandoned."

It is the slow abandonment—the steady erosion of Christian beliefs, attitudes, motivations, and discriminations—that has marked the last several decades. We must remember also that every abandonment by the world of Christianity has been preceded by an abandonment by Christianity of the world, which is its appointed theater of redemptive action. We have abandoned the world for the sake of pietism, or for the sake of moralism, or for the sake of abstract theological speculation, or for the sake of focusing on our own tiny piece of the world as a substitute for encompassing the whole world in our awareness and our love.

I would insist that the new creative forms of ministry are signs of renewal for the following reasons:

First, they are signs that our religious institutions are turning away from their introversion and self-preoccupation and are beginning to take seriously their calling to be in the world as the servant community.

Second, they are signs of acknowledgment on the part of the church that to serve the world it must know the world as it is. Therefore it must find its way to places and groups of people where it has been largely a stranger but where the shape of our culture for the future is being decisively determined.

ソ

Third, the new ministries are signs of a new and saving humility on the part of our Christian institutions and movements. Too long have the churches tried to get people to ask the questions for which the church thinks it has the answers. Now the church is starting to listen to the real questions, often knowing that it does not have the answers, but willing to submit itself to the discipline of the dialogue out of which answers may come.

Fourth, the new, creative forms of ministry are signs that the church is newly aware that it has allies. It realizes that it is called to be radically for man—*pro-personal*. It must therefore welcome the help of, and offer its own help to, whoever is pro-human, whatever may be the metaphysical or theological basis of his attitude.

Fifth, the new, creative ministries are evidence that our religious institutions, despite all their seeming tendencies toward conservatism and reaction, are not so stuffy, inflexible, and backward-looking as we have sometimes supposed. The impressive fact is that these creative ministries are nearly all in some way institutionally based. One of the earliest and most mature of them, the East Harlem Protestant Parish, is today supported by some of the most affluent, conservative, and deliberately backward-looking congregations.

God is able to make new things out of old. Some of our religious institutions *do* yield themselves—perhaps unwillingly, but with a strangely passionate obedience—to his renewing power.

Truman B. Douglass

1984—SOME SCENARIOS FOR THE CHURCH

What is confronting the church in the next decade and a half? When 1984 rolls around, that date made so famous by George Orwell's predictions in novel form back in 1949, will the church have joined Orwell's "Big Brother" in regimenting our society? Will the church be there at all? These questions and especially their answers are necessary if anyone is planning to initiate a creative ministry. Our ministries must meet the demands and needs of both today and tomorrow. Stephen C. Rose, editor of *Renewal* magazine, sketches his predictions for this tomorrow which is being made today. His forecast isolates those areas in which ministries must become creative. He also gives us some insight into how they can become so.

chapter 1

1984—SOME SCENARIOS FOR THE CHURCH

✠

by Stephen C. Rose

It's a funny thing. The people at the Rand Corporation in California can predict—with reasonable if respectfully qualified certainty—enough that will happen in the next fifty years to make your hair stand on end . . . unless you are one of those who believe that technology will save the world without benefit of assistance from the two-legged inventor, man, whose glory is tarnished only by original sin.

If one were to take seriously the all-too-possible musings of computer-age technologists, one's vision of the church in 1984 would have to include vignettes like these:

Vast numbers of old church buildings torn down—with no membership—and in their place a series of new institutions, performing functions that used to be considered the church's ministry.

Guilt removal through legal use of chemicals designed to soothe the psyche.

Mind expansion via a refined version of LSD, giving all who desire it a cosmic vision of man's essential oneness with God and his neighbor.

On the sheer level of trinketry, even if the pre-McLuhan, linear, Protestant-type church were to survive, one could imagine the total automation of evangelism—Christ by closed circuit—with printed media and nondialogue sermons relegated to the ash heap of history.

Or looking at things through the realistic focus of biblical prophecy, the vision might include a church divided in a new way: a union of traditionalists on one side, allied with the powerful, rich governments, and a guerilla-type underground church on the other side, dedicated to the overthrow of a social and political establishment.

On the mundane level of church-planning, the fellow who wrote today's book on church parking lots had better not count on literary immortality. If cars remain the basic mode of transportation, we will have all suffocated by 1984.

But these are conjectures. The Rand people provide us with some raw food for thought. I refer you to an inconspicuous, blue-bound, mimeographed volume with the following inscription on its cover: *Report on a Long-Range Forecasting Study, T. J. Gordon and Olaf Helmer, September 1964.*

On the title page, we are told that the contents "should not be construed as reflecting the views of the Rand Corporation or the official opinion of any of its governmental or private research sponsors. Papers are produced by the Rand Corporation as a courtesy to members of its staff."

Since the findings have already found their way into speeches of Vice President Hubert H. Humphrey, I trust no breach of security will be involved if I note a few of the prognostications.

A panel of scientific breakthroughs tells us that we can anticipate "economically useful desalinization of sea water" by 1970, "effective fertility control by oral contraceptive or other simple and effective means" in the same year, and "new organs through transplanting or prosthesis," the latter already being attempted today.

Before 1990, additional "breakthroughs" include: limited weather control, economically viable mining of ocean floors, widespread acceptance of nonnarcotic drugs for inducing specific personality changes, automated language translators, and reliable weather forecasts.

The post-1990 predictions run toward the feasibility of the chemical control of personality, intelligence-raising drugs, the breeding of apes for low-grade labor, extension of human life by fifty years, control of gravity, and education through direct information recording on the brain.

A second panel on automation considered twenty-five possibilities and agreed that eighteen would be likely to occur before 1990. Among them: a massive increase in computer use; total air traffic control; widespread employment of simple teaching machines; automation of office jobs leading to displacement of one fourth of the current work force (1975 at the latest); automated rapid transit (1978); and general use of robot services for refuse collection, household work, and sewer inspection.

After 1990 the expectations become even more grand: the evolution of a universal language from automated communication, remote facsimiles of newspapers and magazines printed at home, and something called "man-machine symbiosis."

In the space field, a "Pluto fly-by" is on the books for 2023.

There was also a panel on future weapons systems. Most of its predictions fall well within the time limit set by George Orwell, author of *Nineteen Eighty-Four* (1949). It should be noted, however, that the panel is dealing with feasibility primarily, not with the question of whether man, in his infinite goodness, will permit war games to continue.

Be prepared. On the horizon are extensive uses of devices that persuade without killing, incapacitating biological agents, perishable counterinsurgent arms, computerized intelligence, advanced techniques of "thought control," and (thank goodness!) "miniature improved sensors and transmitters for snooping, reconnaissance, arms control."

Other predictions in the Rand volume include: a 25 percent probability of "another major war" within the next quarter century; the necessity of regulative legislation to control and modify social upheavals due to automation; the expectation that food, energy, and raw materials will be abundant, but that "continued inequitable distribution of these assets to the increasing world population may furnish a persisting stimulant to warfare."

It used to be that the word revolution meant primarily the violent overthrow of oppressive governmental structures by those who felt dispossessed. Revolution was a last resort, a complete rejection of the old order.

Today it appears that a new type of revolution is beginning, not displacing but supplementing traditional revolution. The old order seems inevitably to be replaced by a technology and a science which has the capacity totally to alter not only man's outward life but his personality as well.

Scientific humanists welcome the future. They know that there is no limit to the positive potential of the technological giant which is now in its infancy.

Some Christians also will hold out a welcoming hand to the future. The City of Man seems to be on the horizon, and it is not too audacious in these times to claim that the coming City of Man may well be at the same time the City of God.

Augustine, who coined the distinction, might shudder in his grave. But times will change. The secular city had not been announced when the good bishop was compiling his pessimistic perorations.

Other Christians will be scared—scared that original sin may be wiped out (and thus much technology and much of the past reason for the church's being), scared that the new technology may be rapidly replacing God.

Still other Christians—who don't have the luxury of living in the affluent United States—find Rand-like preoccupations somewhat obnoxious. These Christians—Asians, Africans, Latin Americans—join fully with the avant-garde types in Europe and the

United States in saying that the church must be at the side of the suffering, fighting for justice, placing the need of the world ahead of the institutional preservation of the church.

They simply do not see much hope of attaining a stage of development which might permit the luxury of reflection on a technological future.

Their lands are the victims of a colonial past.

Their fields lie parched.

They are not getting any of the shiny new tractors, the big new factories, the bright new computers which spring forth like dandelions on the affluent lawns of the wealthy white West.

Theirs is the world in which three fourths of the globe's population lives (or dies) on one fourth of the globe's resources.

The only future statistics which interest them are projections of a widening gap between rich and poor nations; predictions of widespread famine; anticipations of unbridled increases in population that will, at a minimum, double their number by the year 2000.

An incredible picture will emerge. A minority of the world will sit on top of an unpredictable, fascinating, and potentially "saving" technological gold mine. Seminars will be held. Lush magazines will be printed. Simultaneously the southern half of the world will seethe.

For these people, capitalism has not brought much in the way of economic assistance. Neither has communism. The picture becomes not only incredible but mysteriously revealing.

What is happening is that the technological revolution in the northern hemisphere will knock away all the old props and ideologies, leaving the poor nations with virtually no alternative but plebeian prostration before the powerful almsgivers of the world.

It is all right for a scientist to be diffident about the possibilities of feeding the whole world—but try telling a proud Indian or a resolute African that the key to his problem lies in humble acquiescence to the guidance of his former colonial oppressors.

The tragedy is that it seems to be true. Moreover, that little factor, original sin, the infinitesimal shade of difference between noble sentiment and individual or corporate meanness, comes into play.

The wealthy world isn't about to give up its war games and its affluent race to the moon, even though the aid needed by the developing nations is only a fraction of what rich nations spend on the soon-to-be-obsolete hardware of cold war weaponry.

Further, because of the past, because of a certain justifiable pride, the poor nations are not likely to present a face of sufficient meekness and servility to elicit the sympathy of the affluent.

I point to this vicious circle merely because the church is generally supposed to be worldwide. A certain solidarity ought to exist regardless of race, creed, or income. But you'd never know it. Really, you'd never imagine it.

For most persons the affluent church seems much more allied with the affluent society than with the ecumenical reality of a worldwide Christian community.

This may seem a roundabout way of getting to some predictions about the church in 1984, but the observations above serve to illuminate two rather important points.

First, the Rand Corporation may be able to predict scientific breakthroughs with some accuracy, but it is a measure of the ferment within the church today that no similar claim can be made for ecclesiastical predictions.

Second, any predictions having to do with the American denominational church (a rather small fragment when you think about it) must be made with reference to how the fragment in question is likely to perform in relation to the whole—the whole church, the whole world.

The fluidity of the situation admits only the counting of possibilities.

It is possible that there may be no denominations as we now know them in 1984. Barring an atomic holocaust, wider church union might "eliminate" your particular denomination as an official entity by then.

But equally probable is the prediction that all major denominations will simply decline until merger becomes not an act of love but of self-defense.

Youth are leaving today's church twice as fast as adults. The idealists find more in the Peace Corps, VISTA, and the fight for civil rights.

The spiritual types find more in pot—marihuana—than in the sterile worship of the average congregation.

All denominations may simply fade away, like old soldiers.

We shall witness an increasing restiveness among U.S. theological students. They will be demanding a more "functional" definition of the ministry, more opportunities for specialized work, more engagement on the part of the seminaries with problems facing the world and the church.

Certain denominations may see major defections among both clergy and laity:

Ecumenical Lutherans will not give allegiance permanently to a denominational structure that stands aloof from ecumenicity at many points.

Any Methodist withdrawal from church union negotiations would probably increase defections among that denomination's clergy—perhaps in the direction of the United Church of Christ or the Presbyterians or the Episcopalians (if they remain ecumenical).

It is also possible that a trend toward "unofficial ecumenicity" will be carried on at all levels of the church, particularly at the local level, where ministers and laymen of all denominations and faiths may find more unity in mission and worship than their parent organizations can muster.

Interestingly, the denominations themselves might well foster this ad hoc ecumenical style in preference to a constituency-straining merger route. Already some denominations are working jointly on national and urban levels, but outside the official conciliar structures of the formal ecumenical movement.

The call for more local ecumenicity will doubtless provide a weapon for those who would like to see organic church union blocked on the national level.

The counter-argument will come from those who recognize that, finally, a church which has no common sacraments remains, in a crucial way, disobedient and disunited.

All these developments will take place in the context of continual flak from the radical right which rightfully (!) sees the local church as a crucial battleground.

No longer will it be sufficient to issue volleys from national offices aimed at the Birchers and company. The battle must be fought openly on the local level, with denominational support, or else it can be predicted that the radical right will use every weapon in its formidable arsenal to form the other half of a pincer movement aimed squarely at the jugular of the institutional church.

A middle-of-the-road, cautious, even if well-meaning, denomination will fail to attract the strong leaders it needs both among clergy and laity. At the same time its conservative financial strength will be gradually cut to ribbons by the right wing.

Creative leadership, bold innovation, and ad hoc ecumenical strategies could save what is best in the denominations while paving the way for a more truly united church. But I know bureaucracy well enough to suspect that self-preservation and sheer force of habit may well tip the scales away from the creative possibility of denominational renewal through decentralization and ecumenical cooperation.

What about the theology of the church—or, let's say, the substance of the church's preaching, in 1984? If it is still in existence—taking that 25 percent probability of major war into account—it is a cinch that clergymen throughout the land will make New Year's Day, 1984, a time of comparison between the world-as-it-is and the world that George Orwell assumed would exist on that date.

The potential parallels are obvious. One minor point: It is probable that the sermons will be delivered to a smaller church membership than exists today. It is unlikely that anything we do between now and then will halt the exodus of a younger generation from an institution which it feels is not "with it."

One suspects that two general patterns of belief will emerge. One will be exclusivist and apocalyptic. The other will be exploratory and apocalyptic.

The apocalyptic element common to both will simply be the widespread realization that world history is coming to a head— the powers of good and the powers of evil are growing, a day of reckoning is near, there will either be a revolutionary leap forward within the human community or the chaos of destruction. What will divide believers is not a sense of urgency but the question of how to respond to it.

The exclusivists will read their New Testaments and dwell on texts which suggest that all those who do not repent and turn to Jesus Christ are damned. They will believe that they are the "elect," that the world is damned, and that their function is to wait for the salvation beyond history which God has promised.

Some who hold an exclusivist position will see their mission in the world primarily in terms of conversation-centered evangelism and individual morality, rejecting the notion that the Christian should be concerned with the social welfare of all men regardless of religion and race.

Others will make their exclusivism a platform for a violent assertion of pride on the part of the white and allegedly Christian West, refusing any dialogue with communist nations and recoiling from the challenge of assisting the neutral Third World in its struggle for development.

Indeed, if any Christian group possesses an institutional future, it is probably the exclusivists. As the times become more tense, men will be attracted by a promise of salvation which assures a future life and, at the same time, enables them to escape the challenges of building a human world for all.

The second area of belief, the exploratory position, will not be a bland continuation of the wishy-washy liberalism that has so weakened American theology during the last decades. The exploratory Christians will hold, first of all, that it is simply impossible to identify the visible church institutions with the "elect" of God. Indeed, they will be open to the notion of Christian life as a pilgrimage, a response to a God who is active in the events of history and who came to reconcile not the church but the *oikoumene,* the whole inhabited earth. When asked, "What do you believe?" they will respond:

"We believe that, in Jesus Christ, God has overcome the demons which prevent man from building a truly human world.

"We believe that Christ called not for verbal confessions of faith but for suffering love.

"We believe that man is freed by Christ, and that the process of history is open to a prophetic interpretation; that evil in the world is unleashed precisely when man, in his freedom, forsakes justice, love, and the responsible use of power.

"We believe that God is testing the visible church for the last time, to see whether the church will truly accept a promise of the kingdom.

"We believe in exploring, not in the static pronouncements of static truths. So we are more concerned with mission than membership, with the quality of commitment than the boasting of press releases."

For the exclusivists, worship and preaching and a certain sort of teaching will constitute their institutional self-understanding. For the explorers, the church will be understood as an institution which not only preaches and teaches but also possesses the organization needed for full abandonment to the pain and promise of secular life.

Now comes the sixty-four-dollar question, at least for the members of the main-line denominations:

Are they willing to decide between the exclusivists and the explorers?

Will they make room within the structures for a radical ecumenicity which will be at once a death warrant for traditional denominationalism and a new lease on life for the church?

Or will we see a great polarization between exclusivists grown more fanatic and explorers who set off on their own because no denomination will support them?

One thing can be said with certainty. No decision made by a denomination is likely to save it from a loss of money and members. So the premium lies in making the right decision regardless of the consequences.

The Rand people do not mention a few other future certainties of which we ought to be aware:

If fossil fuels are not replaced by power resources from the peaceful use of atomic energy within twenty-five years, 1984 will mark the halfway point between now and the ultimate extinction of the species.

Also, the urban problems we have today are a drop in the bucket because in a century the entire world will be one great metropolis.

There is no question that man's propensity for original sin, for aggression, if somewhat modified, would create the conditions of a habitable world for all.

The whole world could be fed. There is enough land to triple the world's agricultural output, not to mention the abundant ocean floors.

The annual arms budget of the United States could bring literacy to a world where half the population cannot read. Indeed, in this context, what is needed is a slight adjustment in the human perspective rather than a massive revolutionary conflict of the traditional sort. It is my conviction that the church throughout the world could give the push that is needed.

Now, a scanty thirty thousand dollars a year is being spent by American Christians to move our government toward a constructive foreign-aid policy. Why not spend three million dollars for a real attack? That's less money than an average small college can pick up from alumni in an intensive campaign. The church must be willing to act on the basis of the inbreaking future rather than on the precedents of the past.

But the push will not be given unless there is a "recovery of nerve" in every office of every church at every level. I am appalled by the desperation which enables church organizations to latch onto every "new thing," but only in a superficial and half-committed way. Let the church as a whole choose some priorities and hammer them through and put money into them.

The exploratory posture is not aimed at kibitzing, but at constructive world change. If an emphasis fails because it is the wrong emphasis, let it be dropped. But let nothing begin without true commitment and a long-term willingness to fight a battle to the end —with bodies if necessary.

If the denominations decided to fight the battle for world development today, they could win it by 1984. You'd be surprised how much normal work would still get done within the bureaucracies even if every staff member of the church at the national level were put on this one emphasis. Let every leader of every faith meet and decide on how to cut up the turf, and then let the work begin!

Will the laymen revolt? Not if they are consulted. Not if it is acknowledged that they are, in fact, the most important element in any true strategy of mission in the world. Not if they are shown that church membership, beyond attendance at worship, is worshiping within one's special field of ability by linking that ability to a total pattern of world-building.

Will the clergy revolt? Not if the denominations provide truly ecumenical resources instead of defensive memoranda to their own limited constituencies.

In the last analysis, my title is a fraud. I cannot provide a scenario for the church in 1984, because 1984 is already upon us, and the action that will determine the scenario must be taken now.

Oh, there may be a few possible headlines which one could imagine appearing on the front pages of newspapers—if they still exist—in 1984: *"Christians" Protest World Government Plan* or *"Christians" Reject Unity Plan* or *"Christians" Oppose Abundance Sharing.*

You name it. Christians have been capable of oppression in the past. They have also experienced miraculous periods of renewal. The point is that the scenario for 1984 is being consciously or unconsciously written by every member and executive of the church today.

I have three children who will be in their teens and early twenties in 1984. I would like to be able to encourage them to join a church that would teach them something of love, something of justice, something of peace. If the above headlines are any indication, they'll probably have the sense to reject such encouragement. I hope the headlines are wrong.

DOOR
TO
THE
WORLD

If you thought Stephen Rose's predictions too harsh, too pessimistic, then you might not still be convinced that a revolution of creative ministries is needed to save the church. To prove the point, let's go with John H. Bing, a graduate student at Washington University, into The Door, a coffeehouse on Chicago's North Side. Here we see what young people, the future of the church, are really saying. By listening, by being there, this church-sponsored coffeehouse is performing a creative ministry for all of us who want to know what those who are the future of the church have to say.

chapter 2

DOOR
TO
THE
WORLD

✠

by John H. Bing

"I've met many hypocritical religious people, but few hypocritical atheists."

"The great are only great because you are on your knees. Stand up and you degrade them to their true and proper dimensions as your equals."

Talk. Every night at The Door, people gather to talk. In a former store, fronting on a heavily trafficked street in North Chicago, the North Side Cooperative Ministry runs a coffeehouse. Seminary students or community volunteers dispense coffee and conversation. Most of the people who talk across small tables come back night after night.

A young lab technician at a nearby hospital asks how to get at the root of the inequalities of city life. She wants to relate to people, but the hospital patients seem to pass by her on a conveyor belt. At The Door she has learned about a training program sponsored by the church for individuals who want to learn how to be community organizers. Should she change her occupation and train for the new job?

A young man wonders what he should do about the draft. Others question the consequences of United States foreign policy in general: "What after Vietnam? That will end someday but there will be more—other Vietnams, other Koreas, other police actions. And someday a lot of weary Americans are going to ask themselves sincerely, 'How come? Why does it have to be the way it is?' "

A Negro in his late thirties, embracing "Jesus' sociology" with the same vehemence with which he opposes a "Christian society," tells a white seminarian: "Christianity does not represent the thinking of the Nazarene, because it is not the dynamite it would be if it were anarchist. Jesus said that the kingdom of God is among you, a stateless, changeless society, a society of godlike creatures living as abundantly as they know how. Thus the basis of ethics should be the vital social nature of man informed of the errors of history, comparative anthropology, and anarchist sociology. Man is the center of values. God is unnecessary and need not figure at all."

Then he listens in turn to the seminarian, who says: "I'm not sure we can talk about Jesus' sociology. He wasn't living out a theory of life. He was responding to a center of values which demanded his full loyalty. I think of this center of values as God, and what we can know about this center of values is always in terms of relationship, the direct encounter of a man with another man. In such an encounter, as in the story of the good Samaritan, what is needed is plain, and what is needed is the will of God in that situation. Jesus could have been an anarchist, a capitalist, almost anything, as long as the demands of whatever social or political ideology involved were not adverse to this kind of response to a man in a concrete situation according to his needs."

Twenty-six churches on Chicago's North Side currently sponsor The Door. They believe that the church today must have a new format if it is to attract young adults working and living in the city. As one man who has been taking part in the activities of the coffeehouse since it opened over two years ago put it, "The Door is for people who are not happy in bars or churches."

Young adults who have recently moved to the city seldom attend church. One young woman from a small midwestern town tried to explain why. "The church," she says, "is isolated from the real world. Church people seem unaware of the ghettos at their doors. They care about local schools only if their own children are attending them."

The average churchmen she's met "are in the city as sojourners." They seem to have no concern for the city as a whole. "They are either on their way to the suburbs or think of the neighborhood as it was thirty years ago."

But she's not sure that this describes the whole church and admits there are exceptions: "I've met many churchmen at The Door who have not turned their backs on the city and its problems. We see them actively trying to change things and facing up to real problems—like civil rights."

Perhaps, she suggests, the church is awakening.

Others, though, remain skeptical about the church. They readily admit that The Door is a good idea and that some churchmen are doing valuable work, but they do not feel that this is typical. They have little faith in the churches of the city or suburbs. As one said, "All they want to hear is a lot of meaningless platitudes like 'sanctity of the Lord' and other things that sound good and are relaxing but actually mean nothing."

The program of The Door is simple. On Friday nights a guest
speaker talks and answers questions. Guests have included Martin
Marty, associate editor of *The Christian Century*, Father James
Jones, an authority on narcotics and penal institutions, and Harry
Bouras, artist-in-residence at the Chicago Art Institute. On Tuesday
evenings there are semiplanned discussions with such topics as:
Without a hell is religion worth a damn? What does religion have
that atheism doesn't if atheism has a system of morals? An evening
with Bonhoeffer. The concept of power in urban society.

At present a small seminar meets on Monday evenings to discuss
theories of social change. Occasionally there is a folk sing or a play-
reading. For the rest of the time coffee is available, chess and
checkerboards are set out. Mostly people talk.

They talk about a magazine article that described the activities
of chaplains in Vietnam: "Jesus did not bless marines as they un-
loaded from LDT's and charged up the Vietnam beachheads. It was
a soldier that pierced Jesus in the side. Today chaplains do it."

Others are concerned about commitment and faith: "So you
must have the audacity to accent what you see in front of your
eyes and what comes from within you, in terms of an understanding
of what is going on in front of you, before you can begin to understand either yourself or other human beings."

"You can study a thousand psychology courses, you can go to
every church in the universe, you can read every book, read
philosophy from one end to the other. But it's a little bit like
swimming; someday you got to jump in, and when you jump in
it's all new."

Two other young adults were talking about the church: "Is it
possible that the church could be of greater service to man if it
helped to find out what he is and why he does the things he does,
helping him to find his real self instead of—in effect—hiding it?"

"Whenever people take full responsibility for their actions, there
is the church. The church is groups of people in any generation—
civil rights groups, etc.—that are truly responsible."

Meanwhile, back at the Vietnam debate, a young man says:
"Draft-card burners are not acting responsibly since they try to
make others feel guilty. Truly responsible people, like the church,
take guilt upon themselves."

Walking around the room, you overhear snatches of conversation:

"I am afraid that someone in the factory will put a knife in me."

"This isn't like the town where I grew up where everybody shook your hand."

"How do people move from a teen-age, fast-car, Bob Dylan, self-centered suburban life to being fully mature men who freely accept responsibility for the world around them?"

"I must recognize the consequences of my actions. I must realize that that colored kid whom I pass by is influenced by what I say and do, and that I'm responsible for how he feels about society when he grows up."

"If we dare to storm heaven and snatch back the positive qualities that were alienated by theology and its authoritarian social organization, we naturalize God and abolish him as a supernatural entity."

"We must try to enlarge the consciousness of the man in the street, but he'll fight like hell to keep his consciousness closed."

"The Door," according to (the Rev.) Bill Southwick of the North Side Cooperative Ministry who helps run the coffeehouse, "is not a drinking, or a cruising, or a pickup place, but a talking place." Here one man finds people with whom he can play checkers. Another wants to talk about ideas. A few are curious about the church, and here they can ask questions.

For many The Door is simply a place where someone will listen. "They are not," as a Chicago cab driver commented, "the angry, bitchy, disillusioned people you sometimes find in the city." Realizing that life lived apart from other people is neither full nor satisfying, they come to The Door for a sense of community.

A suburban college student, after his first visit, remembered the people he met as "militant existentialists," wryly commenting that "anyone who writes about the primacy of existence over essence on lavatory walls is experiencing more than philosophical commitment."

The North Side Cooperative Ministry does not claim that all the discussion at The Door is intelligent, or even sincere. The deepest hopes of one man may become the intellectual amusement of another. The most serious person may be the least articulate.

Nor do the staff people of the five different denominations that support NSCM believe that they have a simple formula for modern evangelism. This is not a tent meeting for hippies. If ministers were to preach from the microphone leaning against the back wall, the room would quickly empty.

In one sense, The Door is an opening for young men and women who are highly sensitive to the inequalities and brutalities of their society, and are alienated from the small-town church of youth fellowships and rummage sales and from the large-city church that does not seem to care about the surrounding city. Here they face the possibility that life as a Christian can have vitality and integrity, as they understand them.

In another sense, The Door is an opening for the church into the world, a listening post where churchmen can gain a better understanding of the real concerns of men and women living alone in a densely populated low- to middle-income neighborhood.

The Christian church in the latter half of the twentieth century no longer claims a monopoly of insight or faith. Yet with emblems and structures in disrepair, the church is still found where men are concerned about each other.

This may always be the mark of the church, a willingness to speak and to listen to anyone, anywhere, at any time; to be part of a continuing dialogue which exists wherever men care about what is said.

This dialogue may be between two people over a cup of coffee; or in a heated discussion about atheism; or within a community of young adults who, admitting their common needs to each other, become in a very real sense the church itself on the north side of a large metropolitan area.

WITNESS
IS A
TWO-WAY
STREET

While reading about The Door, a person could get the idea that creative ministry is just sitting around, sipping coffee, listening, and once in a while caring. This caricature is raised by some critics of creative ministries, and it is far from the truth. Gabriel Fackre, professor of religion and culture at Lancaster Theological Seminary, gives us a necessary corrective for our theology of creative ministries. Listing the above caricature as "incognito evangelism," he purposefully sets out to dispel a widespread misunderstanding that has all but scuttled the churches' coffeehouse movement.

chapter 3

WITNESS IS A TWO-WAY STREET

✠

by Gabriel Fackre

A few months ago a group of college students told me about two men they call the "Bobbsey twins."

These men appear regularly at the fraternity house armed with a record player and suitcases filled with literature. The boys welcome the visitors, solemnly hear them out as they spin their platter of scripture passages describing the joys of heaven and exhort the students about the perils of hell, all the while bobbing up and down with great gusto (hence the name "Bobbsey twins").

After the evangelists speak their piece, the students ply them with involved questions about the measurements and furnishings of the "land above" and the atmospheric conditions and temperature of the "land below," all of which proves to be a relaxing diversion from the evening's study labors, as well as being uproariously funny to the students. It confirms our cool young friends' notion of the church as rather a joke, and not to be taken seriously by swingers in a sophisticated and secular age.

Lay alongside this incident another one also taking place in a college milieu. We are in a campus coffeehouse sponsored by the local Christian Association. Through the aroma of cooking hamburger and layers of blue smoke, one can make out in the candle-lit room the face and instrument of a familiar folk singer. At the tables, mesmerized listeners are caught up in the sometimes sad, sometimes fierce, sometimes gentle songs of slavery and freedom, peace and war.

On the walls are abstracts, pop and op, which echo the guitar's melodies. There is poetry on deck, unacknowledged in Lit 301, but here heard with appreciation for its convention-upsetting novelty and fire. On the back of a menu listing the exotic coffees available, the sponsors state their rationale:

In a confused world, youth seeks its identity. There must be some casual place in the knowledge factories of our time where unstructured, unhurried, open men and women can explore who

*they are and where they are going. We offer these premises with
opportunities in art, music, literature, conversation, self-expression for such an inquiry as this.*

These two incidents represent the two poles within which conversation on the meaning of evangelism moves in the 1960's. The
Bobbsey twins' approach is overt, proclamatory, take-it-or-leave-it,
otherworldly. We might call it "lapel evangelism," for it grabs
your lapel with "Are you saved, brother?" fervor, and usually has
its own lapel adorned with symbols of its message.

On the other hand, the coffeehouse style is covert, listening,
open-ended, worldly. Let's call it "incognito evangelism," for the
Christian faith is not formally visible. God talk is the simple human
act of caring.

An evangelism which is come of age will use some of the learning of the new world in which it lives. One such resource is research. Is there tested data which will shed light on this question?

Centuries of mission presence on new terrain have thrown into
relief certain facts about effective penetration. One such fact is that
to get through to people you have to go native. In an elementary
sense, this means that the Bible must be translated into the native
tongue of the new field. The gospel cannot be burdened with all
our western bourgeois habits, architecture, clothing, politics, mores,
and concepts, but must find its way into the new culture in the
idiom and style of that culture.

Which of these two strategies for mission to college students
has taken research data seriously? The answer is obvious. The coffeehouse as an "in" phenomenon dealing with the "Who am I?" question of late adolescence, celebrating in contemporary art and musical
idiom the new zeal for involvement, authenticity, self-affirmation,
and self-expression, has struck a responsive chord.

One other lesson we have learned from Christian history is that
the problems of a particular epoch regularly evoke from the church
a battle cry in response. Thus in the sixteenth century, with its
struggle against a confident human programming of salvation, the
Reformation troops sallied out with "justification by faith" written
on their banners.

What is the tenor of our times and the answering word of faith?

Part and parcel of the secular stance, as expressed by Horst
Symanowski, father of industrial evangelism in Germany, is the
neighbor question. He feels that men are no longer interested in
Luther's question, "How can I find a gracious God?" The most
alert of our generation, and this includes large numbers of youth,

are concerned with making life human in the three great arenas of being, having, and belonging—war and peace, poverty, and race.

If we have correctly identified the themes of our time—the secular, the human—our coffeehouse appears to come off the victor. If the death-of-God and death-of-church people are right that mission today means simply doing the human task without benefit of God talk, incognito evangelism again scores.

Is incognito evangelism the new style for the new age?

We have done some research at Lancaster Seminary in this area, both at Encounter, our own coffeehouse and lay center in the city, and others around the country. One question persists: What are the limits of the neighborly act? In the case of the coffeehouse, does it consist in providing a forum for creativity; curiosity; self-expression in music, art, and poetry; meaningful personal relations; a listening ear—period? Is not part of the very ministry of making and keeping human life the sharing in the quest for meaning? If we are to take seriously the ministry of meanings, can we keep silent about those very things which are most meaningful to us?

One of the most creative men in the coffeehouse ministry, having pursued this work in two cities, writes in a recent letter: "I am getting the feeling that maybe our approach in the coffeehouse ministry has been to worry so much about loneliness that we refuse to throw our faith in the air, joyfully."

To be faithful to the man question, evangelism must have to do with the God question. When it does, it ceases to be incognito. It stops listening and starts talking.

Such an inversion of the near-sacred theme, "Stop talking and start listening," will raise many hackles and call up the specter of lapel evangelism.

There is surely a time for the incognito act of service. That is what the good Samaritan story is saying. The fellow did not come up to the victim and pass out a tract or preach a sermon or say, "Let us sing hymn 27." The story reports that the good Samaritan "bound up his wounds." The act of human care, uninterpreted, is a legitimate Christian ministry in its own right. Social service and social action have an integrity all their own.

But this marks the beginning, not the end; the first word, not the last. Social service and social action do not exhaust the meaning of evangelism.

In short, evangelism for the new age is not monologue in which the world does all the talking and the church all the listening. It is dialogue. It is partnership in conversation. It is two-way give and take.

The church must learn that there is a time to listen and a time to speak, and that the human quest itself is shortchanged if the resources of the Christian memory are not offered in the midst of the secular and human arena. This dialogical evangelism rejects as false alternatives the monologues of lapel evangelism and incognito evangelism.

Suppose the man of today is not interested in our big keys to ultimate questions. Suppose he is a happy man getting along quite well without our religion.

Are we then going to try to make him unhappy, make him feel he has a need he really didn't know about, and then slip him our gospel when he begins to buckle?

There is a recurring biblical testimony summed up in Paul's confession: "I know nothing against myself." You and I and all men are not eager to point the finger of indictment at ourselves. We are ready to ask all kinds of questions, but not terribly interested in putting ourselves in question. It may be that a good deal of the human quest for meaning in the coffeehouses circles around whys and wherefores of existence but is never quite ready to land on target, never quite ready to put the embarrassing self-question.

Dialogical evangelism, therefore, is not only a matter of answering questioners; it is also a matter of questioning answerers.

Dialogical evangelism not only seeks to comfort the afflicted, it also strives to afflict the comfortable. For example, there is much which is creative and releasing in the new leisure. The revolution is in many ways a gift of God to be celebrated. But for all that, we do not simply baptize it. There are serious questions to be asked: Does not reveling in speed and danger for their own sake represent a trivialization and dehumanization of man's creativity? May not exuberance be a flight from reality?

While the skier is joyfully executing his slaloms, what are the wage rates and working conditions of those who labor in the fancy lodges on the hilltop? When our new leisure ministries begin to ask such questions, it may be that they will no longer be welcome at the resorts, ski runs, state parks, seashores, and shopping centers which so benevolently gave a hand in fostering the church's presence.

Why do we ask such embarrassing questions? Because the same questions have been asked of us by the God who spoke in Jesus Christ of a kingdom where joy is not escape; where life is affirmed and not demeaned; where to be a citizen is to be a man for other men, a man for creation, and a man for God.

Now, of course, all this talk of God and a kingdom of God sounds very otherworldly, the last thing on the mind of secular man. Because it is not on his mind, he can rest content with his status-quo world. What he and his world needs is a restless discontent with what is, the kind of discontent that comes from a vision of something radically other—something out there in front of us which puts a question mark over all that is luring it beyond itself to what it will be. The evangelist must speak of God and the kingdom and the unnerving gap between these realities and those present and visible ones to which we cling with don't-bother-me passion.

Dialogical evangelism means to go secular and human, to probe, to listen, and in the midst of a listening, serving secularity to speak of God. What can this mean in the concrete?

Let me illustrate by describing a project proposed by a task force on ethics in the United Church of Christ. The task force has proposed the depth inquiry into the moral dimensions of the new science questions. These relate to such things as:

The possibility of surgery which removes a brain from one person and inserts it into another's skull. What is the ethics of such an operation that might change the memory pattern, the personality, and—in some sense—the soul of one person into another?

The virtual elimination of death by the use of synthetic hearts and other organs, the injection of fluid that retards the aging process.

The creation of life in the laboratory, and possibly ultimately human life.

Prenatal genetic control that can arrange made-to-order skills and personality structure in the as-yet unborn.

Character changes by medical means, eliminating delinquency patterns through biocontrol and electronic devices.

The church is simply not equipped to deal with these issues. It had better do something about them, for they are around-the-corner realities.

What does evangelism mean for these things? It means that our pressing first task is to sweat and bleed over the job of developing some guidelines for decision-making in these areas. The new science presents a man question of awesome proportions which will be more earth-shaking than any of our present revolutions. The process of secularization will advance by geometric proportion when man takes into his own hands life and death, good and evil—prerogatives which the church now assumes to be those of God alone.

We believe that a two-pronged inquiry is needed in the church, one prong consisting of a group of the most sensitive scientists we can find working in this field, sitting down for several years around these questions in company with theological resource persons, both looking toward the development of some moral guidelines born from expertise. The other prong should consist of laity on the grassroots level, confronting the same issues with a theological resource person on hand.

As you can imagine, such human and secular issues never for long remain that. The deeper the man question is pressed, the more the God question surfaces.

For example, how can one keep silent about the Story when some latter-day inquisitor says that we must fight these scientists who want to extend life indefinitely, because it has been ordained that men live only threescore and ten or thereabouts? Does not a serious reading of the Story—the biblical vision of the world's transfiguration in which "there shall be no more death, neither crying, nor pain"—say that we should welcome with a shout of joy all anticipations, signs, foretastes of that kingdom?

How can we avoid the God question embedded in the human question of medical morality? A faith which holds that God has called into being in man a responding and responsible creature will take a very dim view of any biochemical control device which liquidates the choosing capacity in man, for this spells his dehumanization.

The point is that you will not be able to still the God talk in the midst of the Christian confrontation with the man question. Solicited or unsolicited, the Story will come tumbling out.

The evangelist in the new age may be tempted by the easy formulas of the lapel and incognito styles—the monologues of pious or secular man, the churchy orthodoxy that does all the talking but never listens, the worldly orthodoxy that does all the listening but no talking.

But there is another way—the way of authentic dialogue. This way opts for the secular and human arena as the place of confrontation, as the foreground of mission to a secular society with its burning neighbor questions. It moves in a servant role to act out the Story, to be the body of Christ on the Jericho roads of our time.

But in the midst of the human and secular ferment—yes, out of loyalty to it—the way of dialogue knows it has a healing Word as well as a healing work to share. It is a storyteller and a celebrant as well as a listener, a helper, and a hearer. To act out, to tell, and to celebrate the Story in secular and human idiom and setting— that is the agenda for dialogical evangelism in the new age.

JOURNEYS
INTO
THE
NIGHT

Having seen some dire predictions for the future of the church unless it undertakes creative ministries, having heard how young people are reacting toward the church, and having listened to a theologian earmark the stance that will theologically stamp the evangelism involved in creative ministries, it would be helpful to examine closely several of these ministries now being attempted. One of the most innovative is that of Don Stuart, San Francisco's night minister. His work, described by Lynn Fenstermacher, a San Francisco newspaperman, has been setting the pace for new and creative ministries across the nation.

chapter 4

JOURNEYS INTO THE NIGHT

✠

by Lynn Fenstermacher

It is 3:00 A.M. on a rainy winter night in San Francisco's big downtown bus terminal. An eighteen-year-old girl and her tiny baby, refugees from California's flood-ravaged redwood country, are stranded.

The young mother has a ticket that will take her to family and friends, but her bus doesn't leave for hours. The Travelers Aid office is closed for the night. She has no food, no money, and no place to sleep.

A friendly guard telephones San Francisco's night minister, and the problem is quickly solved; he locates food for the mother, milk for the baby, and lodging for both.

Such problems are routine to the Rev. Donald E. Stuart, who embarked on his unique project as minister to San Francisco's night people on November 1, 1964. Sponsored by San Francisco's Council of Churches, the ministry had no precedent in the city.

To the visitor, San Francisco presents a glamorous image of cable cars, Chinatown, breathtaking views, picturesque Fisherman's Wharf, world-famous restaurants, and soaring bridges over a sparkling bay. But San Francisco also has the problems of other large cities—poverty, illness, loneliness, and despair.

To cope with such problems at hours when a minister is not ordinarily available, the Council of Churches initiated the night ministry project. It took time to accomplish: the need was recognized by two denominations late in 1962. At first it was hoped that one of them could carry on the work alone. After investigation and discussion it became obvious that the load would be too great for any one denomination to carry.

The concept of group sponsorship emerged, and a committee was formed, with several local pastors volunteering to run a test project in San Francisco's mission district. When the need for such a ministry was amply demonstrated, the search began for the right man to undertake the job. Mr. Stuart, a parish pastor for fifteen years, was selected after an extensive survey.

The project is supported by seven denominations in San Francisco: United Church of Christ, American Baptist Convention, Presbyterian, Episcopal, Methodist, Lutheran Church in America, and Lutheran Church—Missouri Synod.

Don Stuart's parish is the whole city. By intent, his duties are not clearly defined. He seeks no offerings, solicits no memberships. He simply makes himself available when a need arises. Many times he has hurried to the side of some desperate person contemplating suicide. He has helped sober up the intoxicated, arranged lodging for the stranded, comforted the sick, counseled distraught couples on the verge of separation.

He is on duty five days a week; two other ministers fill in for him on his days off. He works from 10:00 P.M. until daybreak. He frequents hotels, all-night restaurants, bus and railroad depots, and police stations; he is often seen at coffeehouses on North Beach and at flophouses on skid row. Many of these places keep his phone number posted in case he is needed. Volunteers man a telephone-answering service throughout the night. Don checks in with them regularly.

Many people who come to San Francisco with high hopes of a glamorous existence suddenly find themselves in a bare room with few friends and little prospect for the future. They can cope with their problems in the daytime, but the long lonely hours of the night overwhelm them. Sometimes their despondency creates emergencies, but many who call Don Stuart are persons who simply want to talk to someone who will listen. Unless involved in an emergency, the night pastor listens.

The task is not all grim. Sometimes he finds that a sense of humor is required. An acquaintance from one of San Francisco's coffeehouses threatened suicide. The minister hurried to his apartment and found him nude, submerged in a bathtub of water, with air bubbles slowly rising to the surface. "He was still wearing his glasses," Don recalls. "I guess he wanted to see where he was going." The minister sat the man up in the tub and talked to him for four hours—finally convincing him that life is worth living.

This new ministry is foreign to any of Don Stuart's previous experiences. He grew up on the northwest side of Chicago and attended Elmhurst College in Illinois. He received the bachelor of theology degree from the Mission House Seminary in Plymouth, Wisconsin. After finishing school, he served as pastor of Midland Community Church at Nickerson, Kansas, then went to Lincoln,

Nebraska to organize Trinity United Church on the outskirts of the city.

Don Stuart admits that it was difficult for him to leave his friends in Nebraska. "It was different in Lincoln," he says. "The congregation was very close. In our particular area almost everyone knew me when I walked down the street."

To make such a move into an unchartered situation requires an understanding family. His wife and two teen-age children, Mark and Kathleen, are with him all the way. Don and Eunice Rohde Stuart have known each other since they were twelve years old.

What does Mrs. Stuart think of her husband's journeys through the night? "It was a hard adjustment to make," she says. "At first I worried; now I don't. But I miss the activities of our former parish."

Don likes to think of the church as a creative, responsible institution in the city. He feels that the night ministry helps to attain that goal. In his view, the church sometimes places too much emphasis on self-perpetuation. It too often thinks only in terms of the respectable.

Many of the persons Don Stuart contacts during the night could hardly be considered respectable. A thoughtful citizen would hesitate to venture alone at night into some of the areas where the bespectacled clergyman's ministry calls him. In the postmidnight hours he sees and talks with ex-convicts, drunks, prostitutes, thieves, dope addicts.

Well aware that some of the persons he contacts have been or are now on the wrong side of the law, Don contends that the hardened criminals are only a small percentage of the inhabitants of the most seamy districts of the city and believes it is necessary to make even them realize that someone cares. He has found universal respect for a man of the cloth.

Members of the night ministry committee of the Council of Churches feel that the first few years of the project have been very promising.

"The night ministry accomplishes several worthwhile objectives," says the Rev. Douglas L. Siden, committee chairman. Mr. Siden directs urban work for the American Baptist Convention of California.

"First," he points out, "the night ministry represents the concern of the church to serve the needs of the world. Second, it represents a new form of ministry. In our times the church needs to find new forms of ministry. Third, it represents an ecumenical approach to society.

"We are pleased with the initial reaction. The interest of others, both in and out of the church, gives us great encouragement," he concludes.

Time will provide the ultimate answer to the ministry's effectiveness. History has shown that the institutions which grow in stature and influence are those which anticipate the needs of society and attempt to meet them. Seven denominations in San Francisco are working together to extend the hand of brotherhood and compassion to those seldom reached by the church. Through Don Stuart they probably are doing far more toward the preservation and future growth of the church than they realize.

FROM THE
FRINGE
TO THE
CENTER

What works in the Tenderloin District of San Francisco can also work in downtown Seattle. In initiating a creative ministry, the Holy Spirit uses people who are outside the church. Herb Dimock, a Seattle free-lance writer, describes how Reuben Label, a Jewish pawnbroker, was instrumental in starting a creative ministry that can be utilized as a plan by any church in any city. The ministry of Reuben Label is exemplary of how concern fosters creative ministries.

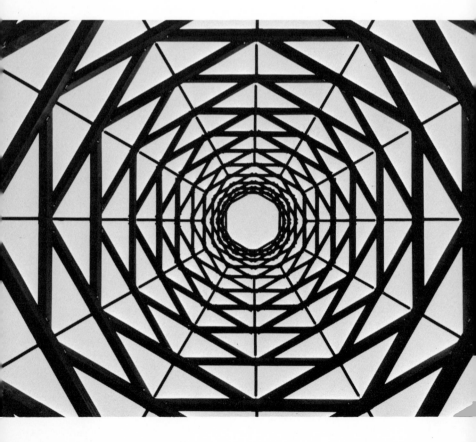

chapter 5

FROM THE FRINGE TO THE CENTER

✠

by Herb Dimock

Two contradictory signs mark the most exciting place of business in the heart of Seattle's skid row. Above the sidewalk, with gray paint peeling and blue neon tubes inoperative, is the label "U.S. Tavern." It confirms the decay that scars a dozen blocks of the city north from historic Pioneer Square, where a century ago logs were skidded down to Yesler's mill.

In the plate-glass window of the former saloon is the other sign: "Rube's First Avenue Service Center." The swinging doors screech as you come in off the street. To the eyes of a suburbanite the appearance of the inside is no more promising than the outside. Ragtag davenports line the walls, a TV chatters mindlessly, coarse men cluster around a couple of pinochle games, the air is blue with cigarette smoke.

But there is also the aroma of coffee, the businesslike whir of a washing machine, and the noise of sharp clicks as young people bat out a game of table tennis. Then there is the friendly inquiry of a person who seems to be shouldering responsibility: "Can I help you?"

Those four words are the key. They cancel surface appearances. They make available to the "people of the street" the resources of the center, the resources of the city, and—most important of all— the reality of a new community.

Volunteers who speak the words may be persons from suburbia: a housewife, a businessman, an electronics engineer, a college student; or they may be a former prostitute, a hippie, an ex-convict, a drug user, or a homosexual.

The practical help they offer to the person on the street is without limit: first a place to sit down, a cup of coffee, perhaps a razor and a chance to clean up and wash clothes or exchange them; then comes a direct assist in the finding of a job, or housing, or social contacts. It all adds up to friendship.

"A guy doesn't have much of a chance," says one of the volunteers. "I know. You get out of jail and go right back to the same old rut: hustling, rolling drunks, passing dope, and planning bigger jobs. The center gave me the break I needed."

Lou is an attractive young woman of twenty-two, trapped on First Avenue since she was fourteen, a runaway from a middle-class home. She tried everything before coming to the center. Dope tripped her at last. She used an infected needle to shoot a leg vein, and blood poisoning was racing fast. Three volunteers gathered around Lou, one of them an RN. They nursed her through, gave her back her self-respect, and offered themselves as a supportive community—the one thing she had never experienced. Today Lou is one of the most effective volunteers. She is also currently attending school to train for a responsible career as a licensed practical nurse.

The promise of the center comes through its power to draw people together from opposite ends of the social spectrum—a power rooted in its origin.

The Rev. Mineo Katagiri is the experimental metropolitan minister for Seattle. The heart of his job is to learn the needs of the city and to help the churches relate creatively to those needs. One day on First Avenue he met Reuben Label, a Jewish pawnbroker, whose store is a place where young people and ex-cons come in off the street to find friendship, job leads, and encouragement to go straight. Rube has an arsenal of weapons surrendered to him by young hoods: switchblades, guns, clubs, chains, hooks, razors— all displayed on a styrofoam board on the wall of a back room.

In October of 1965 Mineo took Rube to the Wednesday Evening Forum at the Fauntleroy Church. "We'll probably meet with a group of about thirty," he said. There were three hundred. For Rube, with only a seventh-grade education, this was a first. "I'm no public speaker. I just talk."

It was a first also for most of the suburbanites present that night. The "talk" was electrifying. They caught a glimpse of the estranged segment of Seattle. They began to share Rube's dream of a place where the down-and-outer could rest from his drifting, with no questions asked, no sermons preached, no red tape. Their concern fermented for a year, and then a group of twenty, with Rev. Jim Reynolds, associate minister of the church, as their chairman, decided to act. They reached into their pockets for money. They rolled up their sleeves to rehabilitate the old tavern, and in December of 1966 the center opened.

Eugene Keyser, director of the center (a former parole officer of the state penitentiary at Walla Walla), became the focal point, the "father" of a new family. His creased tan crinkles as he enlarges on the vision. "Prison does not rehabilitate. It only confirms a man in his estrangement. Here at the center the big word is community. *We* do things together."

On Tuesday evening he presides genially over a meeting of First Avenue regulars and volunteers from suburbia—usually between thirty and seventy persons. Here the reconciling power of the new community is most visible, and it shows up as a two-way street. This is not the middle class bringing its largess to the deprived. The people of the street have their own abilities, and they are proud.

At Halloween time there was talk of a suburban group offering to bring a party and all the trimmings. The atmosphere grew heavy with the greed of things until Ken, a young bearded Negro, sounded off: "We're always looking for other people to do for us. How about us doing for somebody else for a change?"

The seed grew faster than Jack's beanstalk. Unknown talents for art, recreation, leadership, and social organization were released. The regulars gave twenty-five children, ages five to twelve, from the central area ghetto, the time of their lives; and their glow of achievement spread as they thought ahead to Thanksgiving and Christmas.

Volunteers from the larger community confessed privately to each other, "I never thought they could pull it off. They're wonderful!"

Gene Keyser reminded them, "Not 'they.' It's 'we.' "

The center is full of contradictions: First Avenue people giving suburbia a sense of belonging; the church of Christ existing, in fact, without the traditional marks of language and worship; hope blossoming in Seattle's most despairing locale. In the words of a suburbanite volunteer, "We're closer to the center of life down here. Our plush neighborhoods are out on the fringes."

A dramatic evidence of the ferment that works through the center came when director Keyser shared with his motley "family" a case of special need. "There's a young fellow ready for parole from Monroe (the state reformatory). His crime was car theft, but his real problem is sex perversion (with children and animals). He won't be released unless there's a community willing to take responsibility for him."

The Tuesday evening meeting divided radically pro and con. "This is a job for skilled psychiatric treatment," some said. But others with daring born of newfound compassion met later and formed a small group to support and supervise the newcomer.

"What can a psychiatrist do?" they asked. "He's not a community." No one who has seen what has already been done will say that this special therapy group cannot succeed.

Perhaps the face which reflects the sharpest contradiction that is the center belongs to the young bearded Negro, Ken. Outwardly he might be pegged as a "wino," or a "hippie," or a "thief." Yet his performance is the opposite. From week to week he postpones his own plans to pursue what he calls "the experiment." He talks big about vague connections he has elsewhere, but he chooses the real community on First Avenue instead of the wandering, wasting, wanting life that was his past.

The future is bright. Soon to be established is a halfway house that will help to ease the inner bruises of skid row people and ready them for return to full responsible sharing in the life of Seattle.

Plans are afoot to launch a night ministry, through which volunteers are especially trained to roam the sidewalks and head off developing trouble before it breaks into violence and crime.

Downtown Plymouth Church, with its splendid new building, has volunteered to be an auxiliary meeting place. Now people of the center can walk uphill a half dozen blocks, through the shadow of the IBM building, to the church and share in classes they have requested: basic economics of how to get and keep a job, sewing, speech therapy, guitar, janitorial practice.

A Catholic junior high school has promised its gymnasium on Sunday afternoons for First Avenue recreational purposes. Catholic nuns and volunteer priests give their skilled efforts as counselors, while quietly seeking the official approval of their archbishop. Presbyterians and Methodists have joined with United Church of Christ and Roman Catholic backers.

Rube Label's dream has been given flesh and is racing off in search of new dreams. The signs over the sidewalk and in the window of 1009 First Avenue are precise. As the "U.S. Tavern" the place promised temporary anesthesia for the soul pains of men. But as the First Avenue Service Center the very walls are alive with returning health.

TAKING
THE CHURCH
TO THE
FACTORY

We have seen creative ministries to the night people of San Francisco, and those down and out on Seattle's First Avenue. But how does a creative ministry respond to the average man working five days a week? How does the gospel get through to what some have called "technological man"? Newman Cryer, a religious journalist, gives part of the answer in his study of the Detroit Industrial Mission, a prototype that has spawned similar creative ministries across the nation.

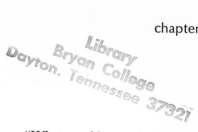

TAKING THE CHURCH TO THE FACTORY

✠

by Newman Cryer

"What would you clergymen talk about to a group of our engineers —if you had the chance?" The personnel manager of a huge Detroit firm was skeptical.

His question was directed to the Rev. Jesse E. Christman of the Detroit Industrial Mission staff. Mr. Christman and a Catholic priest had come to ask permission to engage a group of engineers in a series of conversations geared to problems they face in their jobs.

"We would want them to do most of the talking," Jesse replied. "To give you an idea, here is a list of proposed topics."

Scanning the list, the personnel manager was surprised to find "unreligious" subjects: "The engineer as a professional"; "How does my job affect my family life?"; "Am I helping to make the kind of world I really want?" Then, after suggesting other possible topics, he gave them a green light and permission to use the company's conference room after working hours—if they could find enough interested engineers willing to participate.

This is one way the Detroit Industrial Mission reaches small groups of people at all levels in one of the world's largest industrial centers. Its five-man, ecumenical staff works quietly—but with great vigor—to show the church's concern for people and their job problems.

Although now well beyond the exploratory stage, DIM is still a highly specialized ministry on the church frontier. It rigorously avoids a denominational approach, because it works not only with Jews, Roman Catholics, and Protestants, but also with agnostics and atheists.

The basic approach is to get into a plant and build contacts with men who can organize small discussion groups. Instead of trying to get people to church, DIM takes the church to people. Discussion topics are drawn from the concerns of the group.

To see how a staffer works with an established group, I trailed the Rev. James M. Campbell to the main plant of Whitehead and Kales, an old-line steel company in River Rouge. Its more than

1,750 shop workers and 400 management people fabricate and market structural steel and automobile-rack installations for railroad cars and highway trailers to haul Detroit's best-known product across the country.

I was met at the gate by the contact person, Stanford Lozon, vice-president of the United Steelworkers of America, Local 2341. I was given a badge that admitted me to the place where, on signal of the noon whistle, eleven production workers gathered for a lunch-hour discussion of "the union as a career opportunity."

This particular group was to meet only six times. Then another group was to be organized to consider a different topic. Anyone in the plant who wished to, might join. Many of the same men continued in each new group formed.

Those in the group we visited chewed not only on sandwiches, but also on random gripes and comments overheard on the shop floor. For example:

"The few who really get going up the union ladder have to brownnose it all the way."

"All right, tell me the truth: Does your son want to grow up to be a labor leader?"

"Why should I waste my time and talents? They crucify you for it in the end."

DIM has had close contact with this plant ever since the first series of discussions with a top management group more than seven years ago. Now DIM works mostly with welders, fitters, and other steelworkers in the shops. But there also are sessions with lower-level management men.

Staff members are reluctant to point to any group as typical. Each has a uniqueness determined by the men and their characteristic problems. This year DIM will meet with over twenty industry-related groups in and around Detroit.

In this kind of dialogue, staffers try to get a group engaged in the kind of self-criticism which leads to innovation and improvement. They strive for sharply focused conversation which points the way to responsible action—helping the union committeeman find out how to get reelected and still do a good job, or the manager to see how he can consider the human values of a situation while keeping costs down and production and profits up.

Working in industry is primary with DIM, but a secondary thrust is made into the churches. This is done through discussion groups composed of people in similar work and drawn from one or more congregations. These groups are important for two reasons. First, they enable DIM staff members to explore directly with churchmen the real issues of work life; and second, these contacts help them to gain an entrance to factories and businesses where new on-the-job discussions may be started.

The idea for a mission to industry came to the Rev. Hugh C. White, Jr., while he was serving St. Luke's Episcopal Church in Ypsilanti. During his seven-year pastorate there, he noticed that nearly all the people pouring into the mushrooming suburb came to work in nearby industry. He sensed that the church had little to offer them—that, in fact, the church had no real communication with them.

His suspicions were reinforced by conversations with businessmen to probe their on-the-job problems, and by visits to factories where he talked with blue-collar workers. These experiences led him to join the Parishfield Community in Brighton, Michigan, where he made a three-year study of Christianity and industrial life.

With this background, he and one layman started the Detroit Industrial Mission in May 1956. Later he became its executive director.

Hugh White is a dynamo and an enthusiastic leader. A native Detroiter, he is chief administrator, ambassador-at-large, and co-ordinator and reviewer of staff activities. He makes high-level contacts in industry, church, and government—and still manages a share of the field work, through which he trains junior staff members.

Recently he served as a consultant to the U.S. Department of Labor and as chairman of the Michigan Governor's Commission on Workmen's Compensation. The state now has an updated law based on the commission's studies.

In its first years, the mission used makeshift quarters in a parish church. Financial support came from a few concerned individuals, including the Rt. Rev. Richard S. M. Emrich, bishop of Michigan's Protestant Episcopal Diocese, who paid part of the first salaries out of his own pocket.

Fresh from three years' experience in England's Sheffield Industrial Mission, Scott Paradise, an Episcopalian, joined the staff during the second year. Robert C. Batchelder, a United Church of Christ minister, joined in 1960 to develop publications and augment field work. He edited a quarterly newspaper, *Life and Work*, which goes to forty-five hundred former group members and other friends of the mission. He also edited occasional papers on aspects of Christian faith and industrial activity.

Jim Campbell and Jesse Christman are Presbyterian ministers who had been associated with an industrial project of the Detroit

Presbytery in the working-class neighborhood of Ecorse, a down-river suburb.

Another staff member is the Rev. Philip H. Doster, a Methodist. He chose the ministry because, as he says, "It seemed to me that the church was the main instrument concerned with people, expressing both compassion and justice." Since then he has had a passion for relating the church significantly to the real, everyday problems of ordinary people. His first industrial mission experience also was at the Ecorse project.

Two thirds of the mission's financial support comes from church sources, the rest from friends and small foundations. Presbyterians and Episcopalians provide the largest share from denominational sources, with the United Church of Christ contributions in third place.

From its beginning, the mission has been exploratory and experimental. Some of its enterprises have developed accidentally. Overnight retreats, for example, began as a way of explaining the mission's goals to a mixed group representing both labor and management. As it turned out, the two found themselves learning about each other. Now DIM regularly sponsors overnight meetings of this kind to help the groups communicate.

In some early groups, staff members played the role of ignorant clergymen, there only to listen to voices from the real world where men work so they could report back to the church. Maybe this was because they wanted to avoid giving any pat answers to industrial man's problems. But this led to difficulties, since conversation has to move both ways to be effective. Staffers now realize that they must contribute something definite to a group.

In the mission's early days, staff members hoped that each conversation group would continue indefinitely, and were disappointed when one faded out after a couple of years and other participants were unwilling to undertake long-term commitments. Now the staff works to build long-term relationships with particular companies or labor unions and, within them, to lead short-term groups, involving many individuals, as opportunities arise.

In all activities DIM does not expound any particular point of view, but fosters better communication and deeper levels of understanding among all industrial groups. As one staffer put it in his column in the *Michigan AFL-CIO News:* "We're interested in the amount of democracy in a plant, because we believe that the more people you have participating responsibly in decisions that affect their work, the better the chance for mutual dignity and respect. My job is to help set up opportunities for men to say what they think about the human and ethical issues in this place, and to say it to each other."

DIM staff members are careful, however, not to claim too much. They will tell you, for example, that they have helped individuals to think through their job-related ethical and human problems; that they have improved communication; that many people have consciously put their religion into practice on the job for the first time; that they have led some people to talk about life's real issues on a new basis. But some groups fizzle, and some individuals are not reached even when they stay in a group. The nature of DIM's activity, of course, makes accurate measurement of success impossible.

As the first industrial mission of its kind in the United States, DIM has been a model for similar projects in other cities. One is in nearby Flint. Scott Paradise left the Detroit staff to begin a mission in Boston. Other types are operating in Chicago and Cicero, Illinois; in Cincinnati, in Philadelphia, and in Richmond, Indiana. By 1970, Hugh White expects there will be fifteen or twenty such missions in the United States. Not all will take the same form, he believes, but all will have similar goals.

Important visitors from industrial missions in Europe, India, and Japan have come to see DIM's work.

Asked where DIM stood in 1966 as it rounded out its first ten years, Hugh White said, "We're not sure, but we think this means we are still alive." He is hopeful about the future. "Society seems to be coming out of its profound confusion," he says. "We have been through a period when all the certainties of the past have been shaken. The meanings we tried to construct around illness, death, and other tragedies were riddled with doubt. People have had the ground on which they stood cut out from under them.

"But now," White believes, "we are entering a new stage, with renewed hope about the possibilities of life. We seem to be at the point of a great new breakthrough in human history, offering hope in the 'given up' areas of life and society."

He thinks the church has a profound place in all of this.

"The hope of the gospel now is being confronted with action in society," he declares. "The church sees more clearly its mission in and through its laity. We believe the Detroit Industrial Mission has demonstrated that the ministry of the laity can happen at the local level.

"In the past, the church has been slow to risk new effort as part of its responsibility. We think we have helped show at least one way to penetrate the city of today and tomorrow."

THERE'S
NEW
ACTION
IN THE
MARKETPLACE

Creative ministries in factories reach the family's breadwinner. Is there a creative ministry that can also make a difference in the daily rounds of families as they deliver children to school, drive to the shopping center for the groceries, and face the hectic pace of life today? Frank A. Kostyu, a religious journalist, gives an answer in his analysis of shopping-center ministries. As more and more the shopping center becomes the hub of suburban economic life, the church needs to make responses to this life in new and creative ways. Here are some innovations that are possible in almost every shopping center.

THERE'S NEW ACTION IN THE MARKETPLACE

✠

by Frank A. Kostyu

The church is going back to the marketplace. That's right, back to the market. All over the country there is a new ministry beginning to take root. It can be found in the marketplace.

No one knows for certain how many shopping center ministries there are, although an attempt has been made by the National Council of Churches to bring together those interested in a consultation on shopping center ministries. Some estimates of these ministries have gone as high as fifty or sixty. Chesterfield, Montana; Cape Coral, Florida; Topeka, Kansas; and Phoenix, Arizona, are some that have been prominently mentioned.

There are precedents for a ministry at the place where men and women shop and where they earn a living. In the biblical book of Acts the two marketplaces mentioned are in the Greek cities of Philippi and Athens. These were the centers of public life, which had open spaces with statues and colonnades, surrounded by temples and other buildings. It was to the marketplace in Philippi that Paul and Silas were dragged to appear before the magistrates. In the marketplace of Athens, Paul disputed with "those who chanced to be there."

In the Gospels marketplaces had shops something like the bazaars of modern oriental towns. Here children sat and called to their playmates, here the sick were laid and Christ healed them, here men stood idle and scribes in long robes were saluted. The marketplace is where our Lord liked to meet people; we can thus assume that as he visited the population centers of his day, he would minister to those who came near him.

Today the church is realizing that it does have a ministry where the action is, in the market. The Rev. Donald N. Kelly, director of Agora—the Greek word for marketplace—describes his project at Oakbrook Center in Oakbrook, Illinois, as a ministry of the marketplace that serves as a bridge between the underground church movement and the visible organized church. There is no church building, no liturgy, and no formal congregation.

The belief behind these ministries is that the church simply cannot sit back and wait for people to attend a formal worship service. It needs to go where life is. At one time the pastor could walk down Main Street in his town and greet the merchants by their first names, talk to people on the street on a first-name basis, and find himself deeply involved in the affairs of the community. For centuries, the church was the focal point of the village marketplace; it was the place where people met as well as worshiped, and it was outside the church's doors that farmers and craftsmen gathered to sell and trade their goods. Today it is different. Very different! In the urban complexes the church has separated from the people. A minister may know a few individuals who attend his church, but if he speaks to everyone on the street he is regarded as some kind of nut. So today if a person on a shopping trip had a problem that faced him, he probably would not take it to church the following Sunday. More than likely he would not even go.

Don Kelly meets people where they are and tries to help them. On a recent weekday morning an executive stopped in at Agora in the professional building. He said, "I just fired a bookkeeper for stealing. He had been with us for twenty-five years. How do I know that I did the right thing?"

Salesclerks who squabble among themselves, a secretary who has been carrying on a clandestine love affair and is afraid her boss will find out, a stock boy who is pilfering—these and many other problems come to Don's attention during the day. To uncover problems and establish a relationship with both workers and management, Don will spend an occasional afternoon working in a store. This is how he gets to know his "parishioners"—executives and employees of department stores, food chains, and small shops.

He is not in competition with the church, nor does he try to win converts. As he describes it, "We are here and searching for servanthood. We are shaping our service around the needs of people, trying to discover what is going on in their lives. It is a ministry of listening, and in this ministry we are assisted by the people themselves."

Don has improved the communication between employee and management. Weekly meetings and seminars are held at Agora or the Executive Plaza office building to talk over and resolve problems, to become acquainted, to promote friendships, and to share solutions for perplexing confrontations. Don has been able to aid executives whose lives feel the stress of pressures from offices located in such big cities as New York, Cleveland, or Chicago. Men who never see the chief company executive but are called upon to make significant decisions, who sell the product and services of a corporation, turn to Don.

Recently Mr. Kelly worked with a firm that invited him to serve as a consultant to help "humanize the work scene." A team including twenty-three people, among them truck drivers, a foreman, a personnel executive, and top-level management, held a number of meetings. At first Don did not let the executives talk, but made them listen to their employees. Through his efforts he has shown that all too many businessmen thoughtlessly care little about the effect their decisions have upon the homes and personal lives of those with whom they associate. Their concern is with efficiency and profit. So Don is asking questions, and questions are asked of him.

"I am trying to effect change, but I would like to see more of it. The church is finally moving out from the cathedral to the people. I don't think the day of the residential congregation is dead, at least not yet, but there is a need to break down the four walls. Getting and maintaining contact with people is the biggest single problem the church faces. I can't in my ministry come up with pat answers. There is an answer, but it is not pat. You find it in Christ."

Like everywhere else, in the marketplace one finds sin, death, loneliness, frustration, heartache, alienation, and suffering. It is significant that the church is represented in the market to help individuals handle the main issues of day-by-day living. Agora is an expression of the renewed involvement of religion with the world. There are other exciting marketplace ministries.

The Salt Cellar in the lower level of a complex of 124 shops in Northland Shopping Center in suburban Detroit ministers to 5,000 young people who go to Northland on a normal Saturday. Some of these bound down the escalator to the Salt Cellar. The Cellar has been attracting the long-hair type of young people. One of the sponsoring pastors is the Rev. James Garrison, pastor of St. Peter's Lutheran Church.

Perhaps because the young people frequent the Salt Cellar, it has grown bolder in appearance. At first it could pass for a reading room with modern furniture, clean walls, and photo exhibits. Now pop art that berates the status symbols meets the visitor. Responding to the new look, embarrassed Northland officials have repeatedly asked that curtains be drawn when the poster-plastered Salt Cellar fills up with "sloppy teens." Some shoppers and merchants have even tried to close the new ministry.

The original intent of the Northland marketplace ministry was not unlike that at Oakbrook—to be an egghead-type place where clergy and adults might swap ideas, problems, and solutions with suburban sophisticates. There were to be cultural exchanges, creative speakers, and discussion of the arts—among adults. But the teens came. Now those who are associated in directing the Cellar program realize that if they only reach the teens they are getting a great deal done.

The ministry, which takes place daily from 3 to 6 P.M. and Saturdays, features unprogrammed talk and discussion-starting films such as *Parable* and *Very Nice, Very Nice.*

The Salt Cellar gets its name from Jesus' Sermon on the Mount, "You are the salt of the earth." Jesus prefaced this remark with the warning that the disciples should be ready to face persecution, that efforts to evangelize would not always be accepted with a favorable response—whether those ministered to had long or short hair, were in church or at the market.

There are evidences that the Salt Cellar ministry has taken hold. Paul, for example, was an unusual suburban teen-ager—he would skip school, engage in vandalism, smoke, wear his hair long, and barely make passing grades. He also enjoyed murdering the king's English. Said the Rev. Clayton Reaser, pastor of Prince of Glory Church in Madison Heights and a member of the Cellar steering committee, "Paul is different. He still has long hair and wears the same kind of clothes, but today he is getting A's and B's. He has a part-time job on a sanitation truck in one of Detroit's toughest slums, and now he wants to move into this community and join a local community organization. When Paul comes to the Salt Cellar he comes to talk—seriously. He talks about Vietnam, education, prejudice, and the faults of suburbia as well as the ghetto.

"One day we asked Paul what happened to him. He said he didn't know. We asked him what he thought had helped him and he answered, 'The Cellar.' "

Here in the marketplace the nonsocial and sometimes antisocial young people have expressed themselves, gained a fresh image of religion and adults, and developed insights into themselves and their relationships. So the ministry to the marketplace is succeeding—that is, if its enemies do not choke it off.

Serving shoppers is not confined to Protestants only. In New England's largest retail complex—Northshore—located on routes 128 and 114 in Peabody, Massachusetts, there is a religious center known as The Carmelites. Here is located St. Therese's Chapel, a Catholic information center, gift shop, and bookstore.

The bookstore is on the top level, while underneath it is an attractive T-shaped house of worship in the low-rent, basement section of the center.

The spokesman and practitioner of the philosophy that the church must be "where the action is" is Father Joel J. Schevers, Order of the Carmelites, who merchandises religion to the marketplace in modern style.

Father Schevers points out that the shopping center is a way of life today. Some people spend the day there, some window-shop, eat lunch, sit in the sun, or watch a movie. There is room for eight thousand cars at Northshore, and some twenty-five thousand people stop at the center each day. The rent for the shopping-center ministry costs the Carmelites $27,000 per year, most of which is met by the sale of books. The average contribution at the daily Mass is eight cents.

"The church cannot afford to sit back and wait for people to come," said Father Schevers. "I feel we should adopt the concept that the people are doing the best they can and play it by ear. If we do not adapt ourselves to the needs of the time, then events will pass us."

Father Schevers has strong support for the Catholic Church's ministry in the center. Some women plan their marketing around the daily noon Mass. Over two hundred persons attend the Mass at 4:30 P.M. each day but Sunday, when many of the people from the industrial plants stop in. Father Schevers, unlike many clergymen, has no parking problems, for there is plenty of room for all his worshipers. He is pleased that twelve thousand share in communion each month. However, the ministry is not to be construed as a parish. "We are not a parish," said Father Schevers. "Rather, we supplement the work of parishes."

The priest has a quiet sense of pride in being known throughout the Carmelite community as the "pushcart padre." He feels that he has succeeded in identifying himself and the chapel as welcome mats for people in a hurry, for the elderly, and for people in need of a priest but reluctant to ring a rectory doorbell. Scores of shopping-center workers, of which there are thirty-five hundred at

Northshore, visit The Carmelites at noon, during the coffee break, or when they need help. A priest is available for confession any time during the day. Counseling has become the second most important responsibility, next to that of administering the sacraments.

The Carmelite fathers work with each person who comes to them for help. They make every attempt to restore confidence and strength, and then refer the person to the parish priest. Persons interested in the Catholic faith receive instruction at St. Therese's regular inquiry classes. They are then referred to the parish priest for the final lessons and subsequent reception into the church. Father Schevers has turned down requests for the performance of marriages, baptisms, and funerals.

The ministry at Northland often assumes an ecumenical flavor. A United Church of Christ church brings its confirmation class to the center every few months, the Baptist divinity school uses the chapel's lending library, adults and young people of area Episcopal churches visit St. Therese regularly. Each May since 1962 there has been a unity series featuring Protestant and Catholic speakers. Attendance and interest run high in what Father Schevers considers "our effort to help along a grassroots problem of disunity among Christians and to demonstrate that the concern over the problem is common to all denominations."

Unique as the ministry in Northland is, archaeologists at Howard and Cornell Universities claim that over sixteen hundred years ago there was a shopping ministry. Ruins, say the diggers, show that in Sardis, western Turkey, there was a chapel in a regular shopping area. The remains of crosses, a baptismal font, and other symbols have been found. The archaeologists say there is evidence that the religious items and other discoveries date back to the third century. That the ancient Turks may have been the forerunners of a marketplace ministry causes Father Schevers to smile. "We share the same idea—to offer in the marketplace the finest product the world has ever known," he said.

A truly interdenominational project is the Landmark Shopping Center Ministries near Alexandria, Virginia. The Rev. Roger Verley, a United Presbyterian clergyman, is the director. First begun as a ministry to the apartment house dwellers surrounding the center, today there is an extensive program of community education, counseling, child care, and cultural activities taking place.

The child-care center has been conceived as a service to mothers who are employed and reside in the apartment units surrounding the shopping center. The little theater is intended to interest young people living in the apartments who want to link themselves with the theater, books, and music, and would like to meet together for programs that involve drama and discussion.

While the United Presbyterians have invested $100,000 to start the Landmark Center, Mr. Verley has kept the project ecumenical. "Our effort has got to be ecumenical," he said. "Even our Thursday night service is ecumenical but experimental, designed to reach people where they are. Outside pressures are pushing ecumenism, and we need to meet them with a common basis."

Mr. Verley, who used to be a Chicago real-estate developer and executive vice-president of one of the country's largest real estate, management, and development companies, believes strongly that the church should be behind the value structure of society and of the marketplace. "If we take God seriously," he said, "we will have something to say about the development of the shopping center and its value system from the very first."

The Episcopal church is involved in shopping-center ministries as diverse in program as they are in distance.

The Episcopal Church of St. Ignatius is located in the Pacheco Plaza shopping center in Marin County, north of San Francisco. The place itself is used in much the same manner as the early church buildings were used: as a meeting place, communications center, recreational area, worship center, and an educational facility. It is in reality a church with a congregation, built into a shopping center.

In its function as a community center the church houses a daily nursery school, a little theater company, an adult art program, and a community teen-age group. So the "sanctuary" in a week's time might accommodate a ladies' luncheon, a square dance and teen discotheque, concerts, plays, a parish supper, and worship.

The willingness of the congregation within the marketplace to equate Christian witness with daily life has made a strong impression on the community. On Sunday at 8:00 A.M. the invitation is out to "come as you are dressed." The Wednesday evening service is for those who either cannot or will not interrupt their weekend plans to attend on Sunday. It is also an informal service proving increasingly popular with golfers, fishermen, hunters, gardeners, skiers, and other leisure-time followers.

Says the Rev. Charles Gompertz, who is the minister at St. Ignatius: "This is where the church belongs, in the center of things, not stuck off on a quiet residential street. After all, you spend most of your lives in and around the marketplace. This is where life is. This is where Jesus, St. Paul, and St. Ignatius did their preaching."

The Episcopal Church Center at the Cum-Park Plaza Shopping Center in Burlington, North Carolina, occupies what was once a shoe store and, says the Rev. John Stone, draws a lot of people to whom "big Gothic buildings may be a bit frightening and strange." The center has a chapel, a lounge with TV, a counseling room, a storeroom, and a rest room. "They can come in and sit down or they can lie down if they want to," says Mr. Stone. "Believe me, the rest room is not the least used of our facilities either. Did you ever try to find a rest room in a shopping center?"

Like most shopping center ministries the biggest attraction is the church's presence as a spiritual help. "Some people wander in because they've heard of the center," says Mr. Stone. "They may look around, say, 'That's nice,' and leave; or they may discover there's a little more to it and sit down and start talking. Some of them are a little nervous. They think if they come in, someone will put an arm around them and ask if they are saved. They soon get over that. Here's a place where they can fulfill some need and talk to a sympathetic person. What we try to say to them is, 'God cares for *you*, not just your pocketbook, not just your pew space.' "

The aim of the shopping-center ministry is to minister and fulfill human needs in the real center of community life. The church is finally waking up and moving where the people are—and there is no better place to meet them than the marketplace.

MAN, THAT'S
REAL
SWINGIN'
LOVE

A false impression might be gained about creative ministries if a person noticed that those mentioned so far were almost all based on a single person. This might give a false impression because creative ministries always rely on a dedicated group working closely together as in Detroit or in Seattle. Another false impression might be gained from this statement: projects seen so far are results of some kind of action by denominational executives; therefore creative ministries cannot be locally spontaneous. The story of Saginaw, Michigan, and its Night Watch will dispel these two false impressions quickly and also give some insights into what happens when the church goes where it has never gone before.

chapter 8

MAN, THAT'S REAL SWINGIN' LOVE

✠

by David F. Marshall

Up in January,
    Shot down in May,
Well, that's life . . .
    From the jukebox Frank Sinatra was putting it on the line. At the bar were recruits of the swinging sixties, refugees of the lush fifties, hangers-on from the fabulous forties, even a few survivors of the tired thirties. The fluorescent glow behind the bar played on bottles of charcoal-mellowed, filtered, cuddled, aged booze.

Someone mumbled, "Sing it out, Franky Baby!"

Well, that's life,
    That's what the people say,
You can't change it . . .

Franky Baby cooed from the pastel jukebox a philosophy for each person holding down the bar with his elbows. Then in walked a priest.

"That's no priest," one girl yelled. "It is too!" another asserted. "He's part of this new thing in town called Night Watch or something."

Father Joseph A. Schabel of Our Lady of Mount Carmel Rectory in Saginaw sat down at the bar. This wasn't the first time a Night Watch member had received a strange welcome, nor would it be the last. Later Father Schabel explained to the awestruck girls why he was there.

The thirteen Protestant and Roman Catholic members of Night Watch get varied receptions in Saginaw's night spots. From Pee Wee's and the Red Horse on the drag to the bars and flophouses by the bus station, Saginaw has all the problems of an industrial city: dope, prostitution, unfaithful wives or husbands, upper- or middle-class senior and junior executives who stretch a martini lunch into the wee morning hours.

One member of Night Watch, Father Leo R. Lynch, administrator of the Catholic Mission Center, heard a girl say, "Well, here we are on the make and he's holding church."

The watch covers Saginaw's bars, hospitals, and jails every night, a model of ecumenical participation. Members of the United Church of Christ and the Church of God, United Presbyterians, Episcopalians, Missouri Synod and American Lutheran Church Lutherans, Roman Catholics, Methodists—all the clergy take their turn in helping the lonely, the sad, the frightened, the weary, the junkie.

Recently Robert C. Waters, pastor of United Community Church, UCC, checked in with the Night Watch answering service to find an urgent message for Father Schabel or himself. Hurrying over to a dark house, Bob found Father Schabel getting out of his car. Inside was Saginaw's top dope pusher, shook and scared. The syndicate had decided he was too hot. Having gone to the authorities, he was now wanted by both groups, and an anonymous phone caller told him he had but two days to live.

The confidence that Saginaw's people of the night have in the team is amazing. One bar owner called Night Watch to stop a fight. Another called for help to get a drunk home. Each had different reactions when asked why he relied on Night Watch.

"These guys aren't out to hold a tent meeting, you know," one bartender replied. "They're here to listen—just listen." A man at the bar backed up this statement by saying, "The first time you see them, you wonder what in sam hill they're doing here. Then you figure it out. This is where they should be, isn't it? Isn't this what it's all about—this church stuff, I mean? After talking with one I asked, 'Man, are you for real?' "

The common misconception is that people who drink regularly are searching for fantasy, the unreal. Exactly the opposite is usually the case. A bar is a place where what is honest can be said, quietly and sincerely. It's a good spot for someone to listen and counsel.

Night Watch began in 1966 when Russell W. Durler, then pastor of Countryside Presbyterian Church, and Bob Waters, UCC, read in *Presbyterian Life* and the *United Church Herald* about Don Stuart's night ministry in San Francisco's Tenderloin. Each saw the need for such a ministry in Saginaw. The discovery that both had the same idea clinched it. They called Father Thomas R. Horton, a Roman Catholic and now president of Saginaw's ministerial association. Father Horton checked with his bishop, who reacted favorably, and the team began to recruit personnel. After careful screening and checking with other cities' night ministers, teamwork began.

Dean Herbert Catlin, rector of Calvary Memorial Episcopal Church, was the first man out. "I suppose if I thought about it,"

Herb says, "I could come up with something pious about Night Watch, but the real reason I go is because I enjoy it. There is a whole world of people who need to know that someone loves them and cares for them as they are, and they're out there in the night."

Night Watch stumbled and faltered at the start, but soon the clergy teams were making significant contact every night. Each team fills out a confidential report of the night's activities and contacts.

Richard C. Meske, pastor of Washington Avenue Presbyterian Church, tells of meeting a man on the prowl for four fellows who had knifed his buddy. Dick knew the man meant business; there was a pistol in his belt. Before they parted, Dick had talked him out of his plan for revenge.

Following a fire truck answering an alarm, Herb Catlin came to a house where three children had burned to death. He saw an old man who had run to the fire, hoping to help, groveling on the ground and crying. The man couldn't understand why God would let this happen. He and Herb thrashed it out.

Two teachers were talking in a bar when Joy E. Arthur, minister of education at Jefferson Avenue Methodist Church, met them. Both teachers had left their husbands that night. Joy persuaded them to think it over.

Two women met James D. Nixon, pastor of State Street Methodist Church, in a hospital emergency ward. One of the women had a daughter who was in a bed next to a man dying of cancer. Each time she passed the man she was shattered by memories of her husband who had died of the same disease two months before. By listening patiently, Jim helped her.

It's not easy for these men to spend an exacting day in their regular parish duties and then stay up most of the night. Their faces show the strain of the extra hours, but none of them would have it any other way.

"I'm a day people," remarked Father William W. Boli, rector of St. Paul's Episcopal Church. "I have to force myself to go, but once I'm out it's a different story. I was at the hospital when an ambulance brought in a body and a sobbing woman. Her husband had just suffered a fatal heart attack. She saw my collar and started talking. There's no feeling quite like being there when you're needed."

How much the Night Watch means to these men is shown by A. Theodore Halsted, pastor of the Methodist Church at Hemlock, sixteen miles from Saginaw. Ted drives to Saginaw each week for his shift on the Watch as well as for the regular staff meetings. Ted has extended the program into the Hemlock area. "I've gained a perspective I never had before," he says.

The team's junior member, Donald Claggett, pastor of Zion Lutheran Church in Freeland, also drives quite a distance. Don feels the excitement of first-time experiences. Recently he met a man who was planning to leave his wife and family. After talking it over, the man promised Don he'd reconsider.

"I met a lady in her early sixties," recalls LaVern Franzen. "She saw my collar and said, 'Pastor, you should be in your church.' I looked her in the eye and said, 'I'm in my church.' " Vern is pastor of the Lutheran Church of the Messiah. "After a while she told me she was dying of cancer," Vern continues. "She was worried about her kid brother who was a junkie. 'I'll tell you, pastor,' she said, 'if you'll help my kid brother who's on heroin, I'll go to the police with the name of every pusher in Saginaw.' "

One man in a bar looked at Alvin D. Rockey, pastor of Wine-brenner Church of God, and asked, "Man, what's this church stuff coming to? Now I've seen everything." Al explained why he was there: "We're just following the words of Jesus, 'Whoever would save his life will lose it; and whoever loses his life for my sake, he will save it.' "

The reasons why the clergymen are in Night Watch give an insight into the men and into the church today. Their congregations look at the team ministry with many different reactions. Some are 100 percent favorable; others are cautious in their approval. The married clergymen must have understanding wives, since belonging to Night Watch subtracts another of those already rare evenings at home. But, as each states, the reasons for belonging are far greater than the reasons for staying out.

A good example of what is happening in Saginaw with this ecumenical night ministry organized and staffed by local pastors comes from one of the founders, Bob Waters. Bob was in a night spot featuring jazz when he overheard an elderly Negro sitting next to him at the bar humming along with the band. The man turned to him, eyed the collar, and asked, "Baby, what are you doing here?" Bob replied, "Baby, I'm here because God loves you, and because of that I love you too." The man shook his head, smiled, and said, "Man, that's real swingin' love."

George MacLeod, leader of Scotland's Iona Community, says it succinctly: "I argue that the cross be raised at the center of the marketplace as well as in the steeple of the church. Jesus was not crucified in a cathedral between two candles, but on a cross between two thieves; on the town garbage heap; at a crossroads so cosmopolitan that they had to write his title in Hebrew and in Latin and in Greek; at the kind of place where cynics talk smut, thieves curse, and soldiers gamble. Because that is where he dies. And that is what he dies about. And that is where churchmen should be and what churchmanship should be about."

And that's what this swingin' love Saginaw calls Night Watch is all about too.

I BELIEVE
IN THE
LOCAL
CHURCH

Questions soon arise after having read about the creative ministries already mentioned. These questions, in their simplest form, may be stated as follows: Since most of the creative ministries seem outside or alongside of local congregations, except in the ways that members of these local churches volunteer to serve with them, what then can be done with the local church itself? Is there something which creative ministries can say to the local church that makes it, too, a vital, generating center of renewal? Some exponents of the new ministries have rejected the concept of the local congregation as a viable alternative for creative ministry. In answer, Truman B. Douglass gives the following rationale for aiming the impact of creative ministries at the local church.

chapter 9

I BELIEVE
IN THE
LOCAL
CHURCH

✠

by Truman B. Douglass

In recent years we have seen the emergence of a new attack on the parish church. This attack is based not so much on criticism of the failure of the congregation to perform its proper functions as on a critique of the relevance of those functions to the situation of man in the modern world. Many thoughtful persons are questioning not whether the local church is doing its job, but whether it has a significant job to do.

An uncommonly acute formation of this critique is found in a book by Colin W. Williams, professor of ministry at the Divinity School of the University of Chicago. The book is titled *Where in the World?*

Dr. Williams points out that in our time people "no longer live where they live." He challenges the presupposition behind the local congregation that the significant events and activities of people's lives are centered about their place of residence. Their work is no longer where they live.

In our urbanized society millions of men and women travel considerable distances from their place of residence to their place of employment. Much of their education is no longer received where they live. The phenomenon of the student who in his mid-teens goes away to boarding school or commutes to a high school or college is increasingly familiar. People's recreation—an increasingly important factor in modern life—is not where they live. As a resident of a New York apartment I watch the weekly event of families loading up their cars and taking off for a weekend out of town.

Dr. Williams insists that the parish church, as we know it, has existed for only about a thousand years of the nearly two thousand years of Christian history, and that in the New Testament there is no word for "congregation." He points out that when the first churches were built, they were not local churches. They were built at the crossroads of life, at what we should now call the "power centers" of culture—in market towns or at places of central government.

I believe his critique needs to be taken seriously. There are aspects of truth in it which are unexceptionable. On the other hand, some of its premises and implications require questioning.

1. I doubt whether the fragmentation of man's time and occupations, which is characteristic of modern life, actually results in a correspondingly radical dismemberment of his personal existence.

The fact is that, except in cases of pathological schizophrenia, the individual assailed by all these disjunctive forces remains recognizably the same person. In the midst of varied roles he manifests the same character traits.

The jests about the meek, henpecked husband at home who becomes a tyrant at the office are not representative of the truth. A closer approximation of the truth seems to be that the man who displays arbitrary and authoritarian traits at home exhibits similar traits at the office—and vice versa. The tyrannical man at the office is a tyrannical man at home—who may have been defeated by a more tyrannical wife. Indeed, I think one of the most notable facts about the human individual is the persistence of personal identity through many roles and many situations.

There is something in man which is more than the sum of his functions. He is more than economic man and social man and political man. After he has played his role as man the worker, man the consumer, man the voter, something is left over. There is man as a man.

There is a man who hopes and has his hopes fulfilled or frustrated. There is a man who knows joy and sorrow. There is a man who loves and hates. There is a man who suffers. There is a man who dies and who, among all creatures, is able to contemplate the fact of his own mortality.

It is in this role of being a man that he wants to be taken seriously. Where shall he go with the expectation of finding himself taken seriously? Very often he goes into a congregation of the Christian church.

2. In the local congregation the Christian learns to interpret the meaning of life, which is revealed through its crises.

We make cynical remarks about the person who uses the church only as a place to be married and buried from, and in which to have his children baptized. Let us be grateful that he finds his way to the church for these events. For it is just such events that are basic to and revelatory of the meaning of human existence.

Man is the creature who lives always in crisis. These specific crises —the crisis of decision which culminates in marriage, the crisis of new responsibility through parenthood, the ultimate crisis of death

—these are epitomizing moments emblematic of the permanent and perpetual crisis in which man stands.

Every day, in a thousand different ways, he is required to say Yes or No to life, Yes or No to personal responsibility, Yes or No to the God who gives him the trust of life and the freedom that means choice and responsibility.

It is not that most of life's crises occur in church. But if a person comes to church to confront these major crises, there is always the possibility that the church will go with him, in its faith and fellowship, as he faces the daily crises of his existence.

3. The local church is still the most likely place for man to meet the living Word of God and to engage, under the leadership of a trained teacher, in reflecting upon the meaning of that Word.

Even when the reflecting is bungling and inadequate, the Word is still there and has power to do its mighty works. Every man must finally perform for himself the act of opening his own heart to the Word of truth and life. Sometimes the clergyman helps him to do this; sometimes the clergyman hinders him. But the Word is mightier than any minister's power to forward or frustrate this event of meeting.

4. The local church is still the most likely place for the individual to experience the corporate character of the Christian life.

John Wesley said, "There is no such thing as a solitary Christian." This is true. The law of Christ is, "Bear one another's burdens." This cannot be done in solitude. The burdens we are to bear are the burdens of this man, this woman, and this child—those whom Christ has given us as our brethren.

I have known people who seem to bear on their hearts the burdens of all humanity but who never seem to lift a single actual load from a single actual aching back. The local congregation makes this generalized, unfocused love difficult to get away with. Within the congregation we do not meet humanity; we meet persons. Christ has given individuals to us in the bond of our common faith. He commands us to love them, not by indulging in a sentimental bath of affection for all mankind, but by performing specific loving deeds for those with particular needs.

5. The local congregation, in some form, is still the best place from which the church can make its sorties into the surrounding kingdoms of this world and claim them for the kingdom of Christ.

Here again it is the fact of particularity that makes the difference. The local church exists in a particular place, in a particular community, in a particular city or town or countryside. This is not the only scene of its task, but its task is at least here.

I know there are people who can drive from the spacious fringes of a city to their church at the center of it, passing on the way dilapidated dwellings and overcrowded racial ghettos—breeding places of disease and human misery—and see people living the pointless lives of the unwillingly idle, yet never think of all this as being the parish of their congregation. But this is becoming more and more difficult. The church is here. These terrifying human facts are here, at the church's doorstep; and it is very hard to resist the conclusion that one ought to have something to do with the other.

Now this localizing and focalizing of Christian responsibility does not exhaust the meaning or the responsibility of the church. A church that is only local is not a church. But the church must be at least local.

I believe in the World Council of Churches and rejoice in its accomplishments. But the World Council of Churches cannot take me by the hand and lead me to my neighbor and to my brother and to my enemy. It cannot say to me, "Serve thou here. Serve thou him. Serve thou here and him or thy service is empty and fraudulent." The local church can do this.

This is not to pretend that the typical form of our present congregation gives it adequacy for its task. The truth is that vast numbers of our parish churches are structured for everything but their central business—mission. When the people do not come—as enormous multitudes do not come—the church must equip itself to go.

The plain fact is that the local church, so long as it remains purely local, is not strong enough or resourceful enough to deal effectively with the vast collectives and mass movements, and with the problems of corporate guilt and corporate hope of salvation which are characteristics of our complex world and its multifarious society. Some of the major mission fields of our time cannot be defined geographically. They are represented by vocational groups and by widely scattered persons who have little in common except that they serve a major function of modern society—as writers, artists, technicians, and administrators in communication.

In short, the church that is only local is not local enough. Too frequently it is unable, because of its restricted and parochial character, to be vigorously and effectively present as the living church of Christ in that place. If it is to be adequately local it must be more than local; it must be local as a colony of the whole church universal.

Yet the church is also called to be, in a profound sense, radically and uncompromisingly local. For it is only in being local that it can have particularity and concrete substantiality.

I believe in the local church. I do not believe very much in it as it is. I believe in its redeemability by God's action through the Holy Spirit. I believe in the renewability of the local church for its new tasks. We may devise supplementary structures and projects; and these are extremely important, for there are many aspects and problems of our society which cannot be precisely localized. But even most of these have got to be localized in some fashion—in power centers, communications centers, educational centers, and centers of political action—or we shall be powerless to deal with them.

The human person can be localized; he is always in some particular place at some particular time. In the particular times and particular places where two or three of these particular persons are gathered together, a congregation of the living church can come into existence in some form. It is a fragile instrument for God's mighty purposes. But God has told us that even the weakest vessels may contain and pour forth his all-conquering Word.

I shall be gravely misconstrued if I am understood to be defending the local congregations as they are. Most of them are structured not for mission but for life as a spiritual private club. Most of them are oriented around the conviction that the people should come rather than that the church should go. Most of them—including my own United Church of Christ—are, despite all sorts of disclaimers, terribly priest-ridden and clericalized.

We have simply toyed with the notion but have not taken seriously the idea of a lay apostolate moving out from the church into the places where the real business of the world is being done. We have merely given lip service to the idea of a ministry whose chief function is to train this apostolate for its missionary task.

Most of our churches do not in fact view their work of Christian education as a continuing nurture which will equip people for the fulfillment of missionary obligation.

Most of our churches are too little aware of the sweeping changes in the structures and the topography of the world. They are passing on to the future congregations orientation toward the life of the nineteenth century, which will be unable to meet the needs of the twenty-first.

I think we may need new definitions of the parish—something between Wesley's rather vague "The world is my parish" and the conception of the parish as being bounded by the neighborhood or the community. We need some movable parishes that move as people move. We need to recognize as parishes the gathering of members of the academic community around their relationship to the Christian faith. We need some parishes that are organized around common human interests, such as vocational and political responsibilities, rather than on the basis of geography.

We need some parishes that have no church building. We need some parishes with several church buildings.

At the heart of all such parishes will be a community of worship, which confesses its creatureliness and believes that by the grace of God its members may be made new creatures; which hears God's Word, reflects upon that Word, and seeks to render the obedience that the hearing of the Word requires; which dwells in the world in the form of a servant; and which visibly incarnates in its life and action the love of Christ.

This parish will always seem a frail instrument in the presence of its gigantic task. But it is all we have. Twelve men—and one of these a traitor—made a witness which has continued to stir the hearts of mankind for two thousand years. God has promised that if we make faithful use of what he has given us, it will be enough.

A
NEW LIFE
IN
ROXBURY

If, as Truman Douglass states, the local church is the place to start creative ministries that reach the needs of the community, then it is necessary that local churches identify these needs, find out how best they can help, and be willing to take innovative ideas and experiment. One of the most daring examples, when it was tried, was that of a local church in one of Boston's worst slums. Lucien Aigner, a free-lance writer, tells how this community of faith made a lasting difference by going into a new field—housing construction.

chapter 10

A
NEW LIFE
IN
ROXBURY

✠

by Lucien Aigner

Roxbury is one of Greater Boston's most blighted areas. Open trash cans line the streets, tenements with families crowded into small apartments clutter the skyline, abandoned cars block vacant lots, and winter winds whistle through broken windows into drab rooms with peeling plaster. But one Roxbury neighborhood is radically different—because a church took a daring and innovative step.

St. Mark Church in Roxbury is a modest Negro congregation where white people frequently worship. Its sanctuary is tucked between jammed tenements.

Not content to wait until the city helped the neighborhood by urban renewal projects, the little congregation decided to construct a housing project. George Thomas, St. Mark's pastor, tells of an eventful meeting: "Some nine months after I became pastor of St. Mark's a group of about ten members met with me to discuss how this church could give tangible evidence of its concern for our rapidly deteriorating neighborhood."

Housing, it was agreed, was the first step toward improved social conditions. "But what can we do?" the men asked with hopeless resignation. None had experience in the construction or housing field, and their knowledge of urban renewal programs was scant. "We had heard of the city's plans to replace these tenements with adequate if not luxurious dwellings," the pastor recalls, "and these men were concerned about the people who would be displaced by this upheaval."

Despite the hurdles, the congregation decided to move forward. First they contacted Boston Urban Renewal Authority. The big question was whether the church could qualify for a Federal Housing Authority loan.

The delegation left the urban renewal offices with sound advice: Get all the knowledge and understanding you can about the problems involved and build a vast reservoir of goodwill. "This can easily be considered a pilot project," Edward Loque, head of Boston Redevelopment Authority, told the men. With that word, St. Mark Church members dug in.

A ways-and-means committee was formed. Those with business, administrative, or real-estate experience were enlisted. Soon the St. Mark Development Corporation was established, with church leaders as officers. Aided by the counseling of the urban renewal office, the nonprofit corporation got a site for a nominal price.

But one major barrier still loomed large. The corporation had to show its ability to raise twenty thousand dollars—2 percent of the million dollars needed. The parish bustled with activities to raise the needed capital. The excellent chancel choir gave a concert. A stepped-up stewardship drive resulted in more funds. But time was pressing.

Fortunately the church discovered a competent developer who became interested in the undertaking. This company, although naturally expecting to make a profit, looked upon the project with a sympathetic eye, motivated by the same spirit and ideals which undergirded the congregation. The company declared itself ready to invest the additional money needed.

Soon plans were drafted, approved by the Federal Housing Authority, and the loan was granted. With the project's financial footing secured, the nondenominational City Missionary Society passed a resolution endorsing the project and directing its staff "to assist in achieving and maintaining full occupancy of the facilities." This organization stood by to ensure that policies of fiscal soundness were maintained. This acceptance and trust made a tremendous impact upon efforts and gave the final impulse which led to success.

On three acres only a few blocks from the church, ground was broken in October 1963. It seemed obvious that the project could not be completed before winter, but carpenters who were accustomed to working in cold and inclement weather came from Nova Scotia. As the skeletons of the first structures began to take shape, there emerged the usual army of sidewalk superintendents. Unusual building methods and materials, unconservative but tested, at first raised some grave doubts in the minds of critics. They wagged their heads over the structures, and some thought they would never stand up with use. But when the skeletons were covered, the brick fire walls installed, the shingle sidewalls in place, and the landscaping started, community attitude changed from deep pessimism to confident expectancy. In May, the first units of Marksdale Gardens were ready for occupancy.

No sooner was the invitation for apartment applications issued than two hundred and thirty were received for the twelve units available. It was obvious that in order to provide the relatively low rentals ($85 a month for two bedrooms; $95 for three; and $105 for four—heat, hot water, and maintenance included) to the persons for whom they were intended, limitations had to be set. First to be considered were families displaced by urban renewal projects. Second was an income from all sources of less than $6,100 for two-member families; $7,200 for three- and four-member families; $8,300 for five- and six-member families; $9,350 for seven or more family members.

Other considerations were need and suitability. Thought was given to applicants' potential influence upon the spirit of the group involved. The occupancy of Marksdale Gardens is open to all families regardless of religion or race.

The people of St. Mark's decided that integration should be the rule, and committed themselves to multiracial development in the heart of the Negro ghetto. Although this was difficult, it was done.

"It soon became evident how much Marksdale Gardens had contributed to the changing climate of the neighborhood," said Al Brothers, a representative to the General Court of Massachusetts.

St. Mark's is now rebuilding the church, and is adding a community center, including a gymnasium of considerable size. The church has decided to make the center functional and adaptable to the community's changing needs. It will not be built around traditional patterns.

Another church, the Charles Street American Methodist Episcopal, has started its own housing project patterned after St. Mark's. People depressed because demolition has displaced so many are beginning to regain hope and faith in the future.

The efforts of one small congregation, once lost in a Boston slum, have turned the tide of urban blight from deterioration and hopelessness to neighborhood renewal and faith in what concerned Christians can do.

EXPERIMENT
IN
CHURCH
CHEMISTRY

Creative ministries can be done by local churches without having to be as spectacular as rebuilding a slum—as was done in Roxbury. Sometimes, when local laymen begin to probe for creative encounters between the church and the world, the entire life of a parish can become changed. Kenneth O. Mesle and Foster McElfresh, two Cleveland pastors, describe what happened when their local churches wanted to bridge the gap between the inner city and the suburbs. The result was a creative ministry working totally within the aegis of the parishes.

chapter 11

EXPERIMENT IN CHURCH CHEMISTRY

✠

by Kenneth O. Mesle
and Foster McElfresh

The relationship between Fifth Church in Cleveland and First Congregational Church in suburban Avon Lake has been accurately described as an experiment in church chemistry. All the components of a chemical experiment are present. The materials being used are two congregations.

Fifth Church has a long reputation for serving the spiritual needs of its members and for playing an important part in the life of its neighborhood. Throughout its eighty-year history the church has opened its doors to community associations, special summertime projects, nonsectarian scouting activities, and many other programs geared to serve both children and adults.

In the past decade, however, Fifth Church has experienced what many other city congregations have suffered—the loss of members to the suburbs and to suburban churches, hesitancy on the part of new residents of the neighborhood (in this case, Caucasians from Appalachia) to become involved in the life of the church, cutback in program and ministry due to dwindling financial resources. For a period of years these factors had been building up, and Fifth Church very nearly became isolated from the community life.

First Congregational Church of Avon Lake is at present more favorably situated. Avon Lake is Suburbia, U.S.A. People are moving into the area in a steady stream; and these new residents readily join the church, often by letter of transfer from other denominations. They have been involved in church life and are willing to become involved again.

Although the financial resources of First Church are not boundless, the congregation's program is gradually expanding, and each new venture has been supported both with dollars and with volunteer help. These factors could conspire to isolate this suburban church from meaningful participation in the life of the city.

Before the two congregations—the "raw materials" of the experiment—were brought together, they received special preparation. Each church embarked upon a program of study to determine what its mission in the urbanized world of the 1960's ought to be.

The people of Fifth Church decided that they must find some way to reach out to the persons around them. "Have we become so concerned with the members we now have that we are not zealous enough to win others?" they asked. "The time has come for us to get involved with the people in our neighborhood," said Arthur Disbennett, then the major elected lay leader of the congregation.

The people of Fifth Church noted the lack of supervised programs available for the children of the immediate neighborhood. The YMCA on Franklin Avenue, Clark Recreation Center, and West Side Community House were too far away; and, besides, neighborhood children numbered in the thousands! Moreover, they recognized that their own church building, with its gym, stage, kitchen, and meeting rooms, was seldom utilized between Sundays.

Meanwhile, twenty miles away in Avon Lake, a group of concerned persons was studying what their church's mission should be. They heard about "the suburban captivity of the churches." They listened for "the call to new forms of church life." They read about "nontraditional patterns for witness," and became interested in "experimental ministries."

The churches were then ready to be introduced as two chemicals are in the laboratory. To accomplish this effectively, a catalyst was brought in—for this experiment it was Dr. Duane L. Day, at that time a minister of metropolitan strategy for the Western Reserve area.

Dr. Day had conferred with Pastor McElfresh and the people of Fifth Church, and had heard their ideas about offering a Saturday morning recreation program to the youngsters living in the neighborhood. He had heard them confess with sorrow that only two things were preventing them from embarking on the program immediately: not enough people to serve as adult leaders, and not enough money to underwrite the cost of materials and to pay the salary of a professional group worker to direct the program.

Dr. Day then met with Pastor Mesle and the study group in Avon Lake. Speaking on "this church's mission to the city," he suggested that it might be interesting to link up a city church with a suburban church to see how they could minister together and, in the process, to one another. The idea caught fire with the people at Avon Lake. When specific plans were discussed with the people of Fifth Church, that congregation was equally enthusiastic.

Two parish churches, one inner-city, the other suburban, had engaged in serious study of what their mission ought to be. Both had made a commitment to serve the city of Cleveland. Each had its own contribution to make. Believing themselves led by the Holy

Spirit, both had reached the conviction that an effective ministry must be offered to the city if the church is to remain true to its commission to be Christ's witness "in Jerusalem and in all Judea and Samaria and to the end of the earth."

A Saturday morning children's program was to be the initial point of contact. A staff of adult members from First Church offered assistance as group leaders to get things started. The suburban church also assumed responsibility for the salary of social worker Tom Kim.

When asked his views on the program, Mr. Kim stated, "I am impressed with the way these two churches are working together to fill a real community need. I know of no other supervised activity for children in this neighborhood. When school closes on Friday afternoon many of these kids are on their own until Monday."

Others who work in the program share this feeling of being engaged in an important ministry, whether playing basketball with a gang of boys, or taking a bunch of children to the circus, or embroidering samplers with a half-dozen fifth-grade girls.

Mrs. Vera Rook, a public schoolteacher in Avon Lake, became the registrar of the Saturday program. She spoke for many of the staff when answering the question, "Why do you go to Fifth Church every Saturday?" She stated, "I'm not sure why I came in the beginning, but I keep coming back because I care about these kids."

What is the Saturday morning children's program? Simply put, it is a cooperative effort through which two churches are attempting to provide worthwhile, well-planned, well-supervised recreational activities for boys and girls of elementary school age, as well as steady, meaningful relationships with Christian adults. The youngsters join permanent club groups of eight to ten children of their own age and sex. Each group has one or more competent adult leaders. The program for each group is determined by the members and their adult leader. One day a group may make place mats for the dinner table; the next time a trip to the zoo might occupy the morning; another time some films will be viewed, with informal conversation around a table afterward about anything a member has on his mind.

Parties mean added work for the kitchen staff. Mrs. Carl Hartman of Fifth Church referred to this and other efforts as "a very pleasant chore."

The Saturday program was only the beginning of the relationships between the two congregations. At regular intervals the pastors exchange pulpits, an event that both churches greet with "almost like Easter" attendance. Church school classes have visited

from one church to another—and after a group of high school
youth spent a Sunday morning in the city, several of their number
enlisted as student assistants in the Saturday program. Said teen-
ager Kathy Dawson when asked her reasons for giving up her only
morning to "sleep in" in order to share in the life of a group of
little girls, "It seemed like a good place to begin showing my love
for my fellow human beings."

The choir from Avon Lake has sung for the Lord's Day Service
at Fifth Church; youth fellowships have met together and an "am-
bassador program" has been initiated in which selected families
from each church will visit the church "at the other end of the
freeway" on a given Sunday. "This is the best way we have found
thus far to get the flavor of the work that Foster and his people are
doing," said Harold Ault of Avon Lake after he and his family had
spent a recent Sunday morning at Fifth Church. "Our visit has
given the ideas about involvement in the world new meaning for
all of us."

As these two congregations seek to relate meaningfully to the
people of Cleveland's West Side, they are discovering that their
modest experiment in church chemistry is having some interesting
side effects.

Fifth Church and its neighboring United Churches on the West
Side—Denison Avenue Church, Highland Church, and Christ
Church—are beginning to experience a deepening sense of common mission. The actual working out of relationships among the
churches is still on the drawing board, but together the consistories
and councils are exploring means whereby they can pool their efforts
and resources and thus avoid needless duplication. Under study was
the question of whether or not a group worker ought to be employed jointly by the four churches to provide this type of professional service to the West Side area.

The challenge to the membership of the Avon Lake congregation that one or two of its member families "loan" themselves to
Fifth Church for one year, teaching in the church school or working with the youth fellowship or singing in the choir, met with no
response. But another couple from another church—Perry and
Florence Holm of the North Olmsted church—heard of the challenge through the ecclesiastical grapevine and volunteered for service in Fifth Church's church school. Mr. Holm was assigned a
class of third- and fourth-graders. The class enrollment was two.
Examining the records of the Saturday program, he discovered that
there were children in the neighborhood who had no church affilia-
tion. When they were invited to share in the Sunday church school,

ten accepted the invitation! Reflecting on their experiences in the suburbs as contrasted with service in the city, Mrs. Holm made two observations: "This is the first time I've taught an older child who has never been to church before. . . . It's wonderful to have been accepted as we have been by the other members of the church. There's a real joy in this new venture."

It is too early to make any final evaluations, but this much can be said. As a result of its relationship to a sister church in the suburbs, one city church has been able to reach out to touch the lives of some children in its neighborhood in a way that the city church could not have done before.

As a consequence of its relationship to a sister church in the city, a suburban church has had the opportunity to experience direct involvement in the life of the city in a way that the suburban church could not have done before. Through a shared ministry both churches have been strengthened, and each has gained a new appreciation for the work the other is doing.

"Without active participation in mission a church can easily get hung up on the mistaken notion that sending money to the denominational office fulfills its commission to be a reconciler among men," says Bill Scott, chairman of the board of missions of Avon Lake Church and faithful Saturday program staff member from the start. "If we have learned anything at all from our work together over the last few years, it is that there is no such thing as 'an established church' in the suburbs and 'a mission church' downtown—both are established, and both are mission; and the mission of both is the same—'to be servants of God in the service of men.' Vera Rook once told me she had always wanted to be a missionary," he concluded. "Now she is one."

If any more chemicals are added—new ministries, new forms, new dimensions—who can say what the results may be? There may be the rush of a mighty wind and tongues of fire; through the insights gained in this and other experimental ministries, the disciples of Christ may yet find the words in the language of the people to tell of "the mighty works of God."

THE SPRING
OF
NEW
CHURCH LIFE

So often, the criticism is heard from laymen and clergy alike: "This idea of creative ministries, of new ministries, is a good one, but what does it mean for my church? I doubt if it could change us much." The answer to this criticism is found only in the trying. Whether in Boston, Cleveland, or Anywhere, U.S.A., a ministry is only as creative as the church's fellowship is willing to let the Holy Spirit make it creative. William Wineke, a religious journalist, describes one local church that has made a difference in its community and also in itself by letting the Holy Spirit bring about through it a creative ministry.

chapter 12

THE SPRING OF NEW CHURCH LIFE

✠

by William R. Wineke

The air conditioner of a local church in Silver Spring, Maryland, sits unused in the church basement; but thirty families who once lived in rat-infested shacks are now housed in decent homes.

The sanctuary of this United Church of Christ congregation, located in a wealthy "bedroom community" neighboring Washington, D.C., is one of the least imposing buildings in town; but it is functional enough to house both a teen-age coffeehouse and a symphony orchestra.

Among its members are Washington businessmen, politicians, physicians, and attorneys—the elite of Silver Spring society; and one of these laymen was personally responsible for the enactment of a fair-housing law in Montgomery County.

The congregation boasts of four choirs, one of which toured Europe and sang at Expo '67; it boasts also of a sewing class in which forty poor mothers learned to make dresses.

Christ Church is a suburban church with a difference. You might call it a local church with a mission. "We're not perfect, but we aren't afraid to break loose from the past," says the Rev. Robert Marston, senior minister of Christ Church since 1960. Mr. Marston takes obvious delight in goading his congregation out of the church building and into social action programs.

The most impressive program is Emergency Homes, Inc., founded a few years ago by a group of lay men and women who were shocked to find families in their midst living in squalor. Emergency Homes provides a comprehensive rent supplement service for poor families; in addition they give such services as job counseling, economic advice, and training in homemaking techniques.

Since 1965 the group has found homes for thirty families. Although the program was begun at Christ Church, ten other Silver Spring churches now participate, each one underwriting the rent of one family.

"Our families have a double problem," says Mrs. David Scull, secretary of Emergency Homes. "They are poor, and frequently they have trouble managing the little money they have. When we accept a family for the program, we first find it a decent place in which to live—no easy task if the family has seven children and an aged grandmother to house. But then we also try to help in other ways. One of our board members is a professional social worker, and she works almost full time counseling the families on how to make the most of their limited funds. "If you put a person in a better home and then give him no other help, you only perpetuate his dependence on you," she suggests.

At the same time board members of Emergency Homes are sensitive to suggestions that their program could be paternalistic. They have initiated meetings with the families being helped, to discover recommendations for making the program more effective. Perhaps the most notable achievement of Emergency Homes is that it has proved inadequate housing need not be endured by a prosperous community. This year the Montgomery County Council initiated a public-housing rent supplement program patterned after Emergency Homes.

Nevertheless, the waiting list of families wishing to come under the Emergency Homes program is long. That's why the church has not installed its air conditioner.

"When I say that a big issue in the church is whether we should air condition the building, I know that I sound like the epitome of suburban littleness," Mr. Marston says. "A businessman gave us a used air conditioner—and we sure could use it. During the summer the temperature in the sanctuary can rise to one hundred degrees.

"But when we consider spending the money to install the air conditioner our members start pointing out how many families we could house for the same amount of money. This kind of argument comes up every time there is a decision to be made about money, and has gone on for ten years. The members of our church simply won't let the church spend money on itself, for new carpets or comfortable pews, unless they are convinced that the need is essential."

Emergency Homes is only one program of the church; but its impact has influenced decisions in other areas of church life, and private decisions by individual members.

For example, the late David Scull, with his wife, was one of the founders of Emergency Homes. A Silver Spring realtor, Mr. Scull was the first president of the program, and was instrumental in cutting the red tape necessary to make sure families found better homes.

When Mr. Scull was elected to the Montgomery County Council, one of his first acts was to provide the winning vote for a
county open-housing ordinance, the most comprehensive ordinance
in the nation. Mr. Scull, a Republican, joined with three Democrats
on the council to adopt the ordinance by a 4–3 vote.

A unique feature of the law is a quota feature written by Mr.
Scull, inspired, in part, by his experience in talking to people about
homes for the poor. The quota feature states that if 10 percent of
the units in a given housing project, such as an apartment building, are occupied by members of any one minority group, the owner
is presumed to be complying with the law against discrimination,
and the burden of proof that he isn't shifts to the person who is
charging discrimination.

"I've talked to persons throughout the county," Mr. Scull said,
"and the impression I get—backed up by a professional survey I've
taken—is that most people aren't against living with minority
groups, but they are afraid their entire neighborhood will become a
ghetto. The quota feature eliminates this fear, but at the same time
it guarantees that a significant portion of the housing in the county
will be truly open to anyone."

Nevertheless, an open-housing law in a southern county that
borders on a Negro slum is a bold step—too bold for some.

"Since the law was passed," Mr. Scull continued, "I have frequently been awakened at 3:00 A.M. by people who call and then
hang up. Someone shot a bullet through my office window. My wife
and I have found four and five subscriptions to a single magazine
entered in our names—unpaid for, of course. One day a truckload
of railroad ties was delivered to my home—someone had called the
company and ordered them in my name."

The significance of the churches in Mr. Scull's estimation is not
that they inspired him to work for fair-housing legislation, but that
they helped create the necessary opinion climate in Montgomery
County to make it possible for him, as a politician, to support such
legislation. He said, "It seems to me that the job of the church is
to raise the moral issues, to help build understanding of the need
for fair-housing laws and the justice of such laws. Too often churchmen come to me and demand that I take a moral stand on an issue
as a political leader. What they don't understand is that if a man
is going to be a leader, he has to have someone to lead. Any politician can commit political suicide, but that doesn't get laws passed."

If the success of Emergency Homes helped make possible action
for housing on the part of Montgomery County government, it also

influenced the activities of other churches in Silver Spring. As members of Christ Church became increasingly active in the programs of Emergency Homes, they began to see that they didn't have the time and money necessary to do an equal job on some other church programs, such as distributing clothing and making emergency loans.

So they started Help, Unincorporated, a program of twelve churches which operates through the Silver Spring Council of Churches. Each church takes responsibility for a specific part of the total social program of the churches in the community. Christ Church is responsible for the housing efforts of all the churches. Help, Unincorporated, uses a common answering service. When someone calls for aid, his call is referred to the proper church, which is organized to take immediate action.

Help, Unincorporated, was only a start, for as the church members became personally involved in the lives of the poor, they began to see new ways in which they could share their skills. For example, many of the suburban housewives know how to sew, but most of them sew only as a hobby or as a "creative outlet." Their viewpoint concerning the worth of their hobby changed when they met women who had never learned the craft.

As a result more than one hundred volunteer teachers from eleven Montgomery County Protestant and Roman Catholic churches established a sewing class at Christ Church. The Thursday morning sewing lessons climax with a fashion show, in which the students model the dresses they have created.

While the sewing lessons are going on, other churchwomen conduct a nursery school in the church classrooms for the children of the students. The impact of the sewing program goes far. "My student became so excited about the dress she was making that she signed up for an adult education class so she could learn to read the instructions on patterns!" one impressed teacher exclaims.

Other classes, in neighboring churches, have included a charm and beauty school and a cooking course. A new series on child care is in process.

An important by-product of the classes is that the teachers find themselves driving their students home, sharing ideas about child-raising, discovering that they have more in common with those they started out to "help" than they had previously imagined.

In most programs of the parish, congregational identity soon gives way to ecumenical action. "Programs like Emergency Homes and Help become ecumenical because by their very nature they require the cooperation of other organizations," Mr. Marston reflects. "We find that the more we work together on programs like these, the more opportunity we have for other joint activities."

Church members also work with nonchurch organizations. About forty of the church's laymen have established a program to work with dropouts in the District of Columbia school system, in cooperation with agencies there.

But other church programs remain within the one congregation because there would be little gain in ecumenical action. The teenagers' coffeehouse, "The Real Dirt," is an example. Located in the church basement, the coffeehouse attracts young people from all churches, and from no church. "We don't try to make the coffeehouse a part of our educational program, or a device to 'reach' the kids and manipulate them into doing something we want done," Mr. Marston says. "We just make it available to anyone who wants to come. I think kids need a place where they can be left alone to talk or listen to records, or to do what else they want to do.

"Some of the kids take part in other church activities and some don't. We think we are providing a real service just by furnishing something that is theirs, something that allows them to relax without requiring them to join in another activity."

Emergency Homes, Help, guitar-strumming teen-agers in dimly lighted coffeehouses—groups like these would seem to be part of an experimental church rather than of an established congregation. They are; yet Christ Church is a wealthy, successful congregation too.

The sanctuary of the church is simple, but it is far from being only a store front. Many of its fifteen hundred members are committed to the social activities of the church, but others come because they like the preaching. The choirs have no shortage of members. The congregation's music director, Alfred J. Neumann, composes operas that are performed as part of worship services. The church school enrollment is high. Young people flock to the youth groups. Sunday services are well attended.

"The thing we have found here is that as our church takes stands on social issues and becomes involved in helping people to find homes or in working for open-occupancy laws, the traditional activities of the congregation prosper," Mr. Marston says.

This is not to say that the church is free of problems or of inconsistencies. For example, few of the persons helped by the congregation's social action programs are members of the church. Several church members have suggested that the poor probably wouldn't feel "comfortable" in the mildly intellectual climate of the congregation's worship and social activities. Possibly they are correct. But the question should be raised: Should a church allow itself to become the kind of place where the poor might feel uncomfortable during a worship service?

A second problem involves the needs of the affluent members of the church. As the church has developed a reputation for caring for people, a steadily increasing number of persons have come to the ministers for personal counseling. Divorces, problems with alcohol and drugs, and existential problems such as what one should do with one's life are as common in Silver Spring as in any other suburban community. Mr. Marston is more than an amateur psychologist in dealing with these problems—he spent his sabbatical leave with the Carl Jung Institute in Switzerland—but he is concerned about whether he and his staff can give the help which is needed.

"A question for our church, and for any other church that has its eyes open, is whether it can really meet the needs of a society filled with neurotics and divorcees, and lonely people who turn to it out of a deep need," he says. "If we can't, we are in real trouble. But we haven't yet proved that we can."

Like the church he serves, Bob Marston combines a dignified air of prosperous adultness with a somewhat racy spirit of youth. Sometimes he entertains visitors in a quiet den, dominated by a grand piano and overlooking a shady lawn. Other times he tools around Silver Spring with them in a bright red foreign car, and, while he speaks quietly of the accomplishments of his church, a half grin on his face suggests braggadocio—"Wait till you see what we are going to do next!"

Perhaps Mr. Marston's greatest virtue as a minister is that his most committed laymen rarely speak either of the minister or of the church when they talk about the programs in which they are involved. Rather, they speak as if it were natural for a citizen to be involved in social action programs—yet their involvement has grown out of their relationship with the church.

Mr. Marston has two basic philosophies about how a church should relate to its community. The first is that it should take little heed of what it has already done, preferring to look instead to what can still be done. The second is that a church cannot get too involved with its social position in the community.

"Too often we get hung up on the idea that we have to protect what we have," he says. "We are afraid to try something new for fear we will lose something old, forgetting that a church which is afraid is dead.

"You don't have to throw out the past. The fact that we did something yesterday does not mean it is no good today; the fact that we sing hymns which are three hundred years old does not mean we should quit singing them.

"But the fact that a hymn is three hundred years old does not mean it is more holy than a hymn written today. Sometimes at our communion services the young people play guitars and sing their own music—and they have to do so if the church is going to live. We have to give a place in the church to the young people who want to do new things.

"If a church is going to be free to look ahead, it cannot encumber itself too much with gigantic buildings and grandiose organs," Mr. Marston suggests. "We think sometimes that our place in the community rests on how beautiful we are, how prestigious our minister is, and how successful we appear. But when a church worries too much about appearances, it soon finds that all its energy goes into perpetuating itself—and the young people, by whom we mean persons of any age who want to do things in society, are forced to go elsewhere. The more we try to hold onto what we have, the emptier our possessions become. This holds true for a church just as much as for an individual."

LOOKING
AHEAD

chapter 13

LOOKING
AHEAD

✠

by David F. Marshall

Seldom in its existence has the church faced such a threat as it has in this decade. This threat is on many fronts and concerns several vital issues. For example, take the issue of racial justice.

As the pressure of the electorate began to be felt in Washington, leading to the passing of the Civil Rights Act of 1964, the church found itself in a precarious position. For the last fifty years, other organizations and institutions had remained silent on the issue of racial justice. Alone of all those institutions which abound in every American town and city, the church had each year on Brotherhood Sunday politely given its usual ritual of "all men are brothers in Christ." However, as the need for legislation became apparent to the broad spectrum of Americans, a question began to be posed in their minds. If there is this great need for legislation, then someone had been shirking his job. Who had been shirking? The obvious answer was the church, for it was almost virtually alone in having racial justice as a plank in its proposed platform. It began to become evident that the churches' actions had spoken far louder than their words on Brotherhood Sunday. The church again faced the perennial charge of hypocrisy. This time, however, it was with a deadly difference. The church had been seen as one of the most conservative institutions in American life. A prominent slogan of the day was that the most segregated hour in American life was eleven o'clock on Sunday morning. What we all began to realize was that the church had had its chance over the past century and had not even taken the pains to fumble it. The church had almost completely abandoned the problem to adopt quiet, uncontroversial rhetoric.

This realization gave a very hard blow to the relevancy of the church in the minds of many Americans. They began to ask questions about where else the church had mouthed pious phrases and let its inaction speak louder than its words. Surprisingly enough, it was in the very lifeblood of the churches that the greatest slackness was found. For centuries the church had been preaching mission, preaching that all are welcome in its doors no matter who they are and what their past is. The example of outstanding saints such as Francis of Assisi was elevated for all to view how true this welcome really was. Now, people began to ask why we had to go all the way back to the middle ages in order to get the example. The laity began to ask where the saints were who held open the church doors and welcomed the destitute, the poor, the prostitute, the habitual gambler, the ex-convict. What had happened in church life between the time of Francis of Assisi and now?

Luckily, the churches were able to point to the new, creative ministries as a possible solution. This seemed at first to appease the question askers, but it did not do so for long. They began to ask why these ministries were thought of as new or creative. They began to wonder how really new these creative ministries were. As Frank Kostyu pointed out in "There's New Action in the Marketplace," the shopping-center ministries were patterned after those in Asia Minor two millennia ago.

The creative ministries became in themselves indictments against the church's lethargy. Those parish pastors who felt most threatened by this truth gnawing in the back of their own minds were quick to rush to the defense of the local parish. Those question askers who were puzzled at the churches' lethargy, especially the conservative self-fulfilling tendency in some parishes, began to argue that perhaps the local parish as institution had better go. They began to quote best sellers on how the local parish was captive to its suburban society and culture. A battle began to rage over the relevancy of creative ministries vis-à-vis the local parish.

This battle is now largely in the past. It was ended, and an effective truce was brought about by a group of enterprising and dedicated local pastors and laymen. This group saw creative ministries not as a different kind of institution, but as a different style of ministry compared to the traditional ministry undertaken by the local parish. There were things in the style of creative ministries that the local parish could imitate and profit from.

This group of clergy and laity saw that the local parish is, indeed, as Truman B. Douglass pointed out in "I Believe in the Local Church," the basic launching pad for future relevancy of the church in the world. They began to revitalize the ministry of local parishes by adopting the methods and styles of the creative ministries.

The above description has slightly caricatured what happened. In reality, the creative ministries borrowed styles and methods from a few enterprising local parishes, and some local parishes adopted styles from creative ministries. This process of exchange has been going on throughout the life of the church. The only difference has been that, up until the present decade, it was usually an unconscious or a semiconscious borrowing both ways. The publicity that creative ministries have received in the nation's press has made the borrowing process conscious; it has elevated the interchange to a platform for public-viewing.

It became fashionable in ecclesiastical circles several years ago to open a coffeehouse for young people. Here, the local churches were adopting the style of creative ministries. However, the complete style was not adopted. The coffeehouses were successful to a degree, as John Bing has shown us in "Door to the World." What the local parishes failed to adopt when setting up coffeehouses was the stance necessary for true evangelism—that stance outlined by Gabriel Fackre in "Witness Is a Two-way Street." It was not enough just to have a place to drink coffee and talk while the church listened. The church had to talk back; it had to have something to say, and that something was the gospel.

Closer examination of creative ministries yielded new indictments of the past history of the local parishes. The example of Don Stuart's San Francisco night ministry can be followed by every member of every local parish to some degree. The concern for society's forgotten people, for those who are elsewhere unwanted, is one of the hallmarks of the creative ministries' style.

How effective this concern can be is illustrated in "Man, That's Real Swingin' Love," the story of Saginaw's Night Watch; in "From the Fringe to the Center," the essay on Seattle's First Avenue Center; and in "Taking the Church to the Factory," an analysis of the Detroit Industrial Mission.

What happens to local churches when they adopt and modify the styles of creative ministries can be seen in "Experiment in Church Chemistry," "A New Life in Roxbury," and "The Spring of New Church Life."

Stephen C. Rose fears that the church will become more and more divided between those persons who will opt for the traditional style of ministry and those who will choose the creative ministries' style. In this one instance perhaps, hopefully, he is mistaken. The growing cooperation between local parish and creative ministry, the continued sharing of both styles of ministry, can only have the effect of stopping any such schism in American church life. The problem is whether or not this cooperation is growing and will continue to incorporate more and more local churches. It will mean that local parishes will have to do more for creative ministries than they have done in the past. It will demand more than financial support (sometimes given grudgingly) and the contribution of a few turned-on laymen. It will mean a close scrutiny of what creative ministries are doing and what they hope to do, what the churches are doing and what they hope to accomplish. It will demand that all Christians ask questions about their personal styles of ministry—questions such as: Is this really me or is this only a facade and a mask that I wear? Is this action something I can sign my name to in good faith and confidence? Is this personal life style what I really want it to be? Am I making a difference in the world by creatively living in it?

When concerned Christians and enlightened churches begin to ask questions like these, a truly creative ministry of the entire church might not be far away.